Hello and welcome!
Ich bin der Wordmaster und helfe dir beim Wörterlernen.

Ganz wichtig! Nachdem du neue Wörter in der Schule besprochen hast, mach die **New words** *in diesem Heft.*

Du siehst, die ***fett gedruckten*** *deutschen Wörter sind Lernw*
Sie fehlen im englischen Satz, damit du sie eintragen kannst.

Meine Tipps

1. *Die Reihenfolge der* **New words** *entspricht der Reihenfolge der neuen Wörter im Vocabulary deines Schülerbuches. Dort kannst du deine Lösungen überprüfen.*
2. *Wenn du mal nicht weiter weißt, kannst du auch im Vocabulary nachschauen.*
3. *Lerne neue Wörter in einem Satz. So kann man sie sich besser merken.*
4. *Übe den neuen Wortschatz. Decke zum Beispiel mit einem Blatt Papier die englischen Sätze ab und versuche, die deutschen Sätze ins Englische zu übersetzen. Oder umgekehrt.*

New words ▸ p. 1

Mein **Name** ist ...	My name is ...
Ich komme aus Deutschland.	I'm from Germany.
Ich gehe zur **Schule**.	I go to school .
Ich **lerne** Englisch.	I ________ English.
Unser **Lehrer** ist nett.	Our ________ is nice.

Übrigens:
Außer **New words** *gibt es andere Übungen, darunter viele Wortspiele und Rätsel.*

Die Lösungen findest du im beigelegten Lösungsblatt.

Welcome

New words ▸ *pp. 6 – 8*

Tatjana ist ein **hübsches** Mädchen.	Tatjana is a ____________________ girl.
Ich komme aus Berlin. **Und du**?	I'm from Berlin. ____________________________?
Willkommen in Berlin.	____________________________ Berlin.
Ich **kann mich mit** dir **unterhalten.**	I _________________________________ you.
Sprich mit deinem **Partner.**	Talk to your ____________________.
Jetzt können wir Jack **kennen lernen.**	_____________ we can _________________ Jack.
Und **dies ist** Ananda.	And ______________________ Ananda.
Ist Jack aus London? – Nein, **er ist** aus Bristol.	Is Jack from London? – No, _______ from Bristol.
Und Ananda? – **Sie ist auch** aus Bristol.	What about Ananda? – ________ from Bristol _______.
Sophie ist **neu** in Bristol.	Sophie is ___________ in Bristol.
Dan ist im Park **mit** Jo.	Dan is in the park _____________ Jo.
Jo ist **sein Zwillingsbruder.**	Jo is ____.
Sie sind 12 Jahre alt.	_________________ 12 years old.
Ich kann über Farben **sprechen.**	____________________________________ colours.
Mir gefällt **Seite** 8 in unserem Englischbuch.	I like _______________ 8 in our English book.

1 Lost words

Füge das richtige Wort in die Lücken ein. Verwende die Wörter in den Luftballons.

1 My name is Max. I'm ___from___ Hamburg.

2 I'm 11 years old. What _____________ you?

3 This is Robin Brown _____________ his twin brother Mike.

4 They aren't German – they're _____________ England.

5 They live _____________ Bristol – in Hotwell Road.

6 Welcome _____________ Bristol!

7 Can you sing a song _____________ English?

8 I can talk to my partner _____________ my favourite colour.

New words ▸ pp. 9 – 10

Es ist ein neues Skateboard.	__________ a new skateboard.
Leipzig ist **ein toller Ort.**	Leipzig is ______________________________ .
Ich kann ein großes Haus **sehen.**	______________________________ big house.
Auf dem **Foto** sehe ich einen blauen **Drachen.**	_____ the __________ I see a blue __________ .
ein altes Haus in der **Parkstraße**	an old house in ____________________
Ich bin glücklich, **wenn** ich dich sehe.	I'm happy __________ I see you.
ein **leeres** Glas und ein **volles** Glas	an __________ glass and a __________ glass.
Prunella kann **Dinge schließen.**	Prunella can ______________________________ .
Bitte **öffne** das Buch auf Seite 10.	Please __________ the book at page 10.
Du **schiebst** und ich **ziehe.**	You __________ and I __________ .
Ich **lasse** die Fotos **fallen** und	I __________ the photos and
... **dann lache** ich.	... __________ I __________ .
Schau auf das Foto.	__________ at the photo.
Es ist hübsch, **aber** es ist nicht groß.	It's pretty, __________ it isn't big.
Wo bin ich? Du **kannst mich nicht finden!**	Where am I? You ______________________________ !
Schau, **das bin ich.**	Look, ____________________ .

2 Picture crossword

Füge das richtige Wort in die Lücken ein.

Across →

3 

4 

7 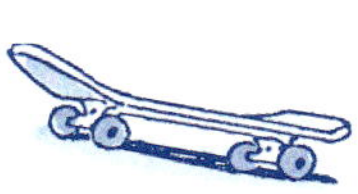

9 

Down ↓

1 

2 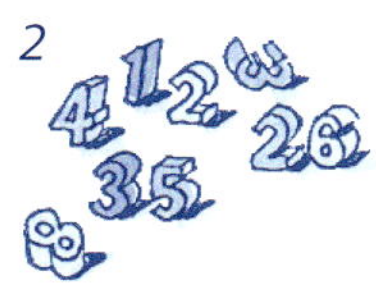

4 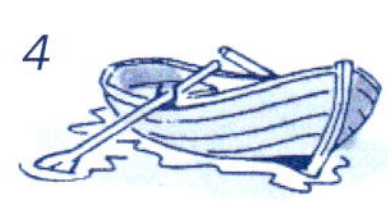

6 

5 

8 

New words ▸ p. 11

Kannst du sie **auf** dem **Bild** sehen?	Can you see her ______ the ____________________ ?
Ich glaube, das ist Sophie.	____________________ that's Sophie.
Ja, **das ist richtig**.	Yes, ____________________ .
Sophies Zimmer ist **sehr schön**.	Sophie's room is ____________________ .
Sophie, **du kannst das Baby nehmen**.	Sophie, ______________________________ .
Und **du kannst mir helfen**, Papa.	And ______________________________ , Dad.
Es ist sehr schön **hier drinnen**.	It's very nice ____________________ .
Ich bin Sophie und **wer bist du**?	I'm Sophie and ______________________________ ?
Sophie, das ist dein Zimmer **da**.	Sophie, that's your room ____________________ .

3 Spot the mistakes

In jedem Satz gibt es zwei Fehler. Unterstreiche und korrigiere sie.

1 Ananda is form Bristol, but Sophie is nju in Bristol. from ____________ ____________

2 Dan and Jo are twinn brothers. They'er 12 years old. ____________ ____________

3 I laufh when I'm heppy. ____________ ____________

4 17 Cotham Park Road is a bigg old hause in Bristol. ____________ ____________

5 When the house is empti, Prunella iss happy. ____________ ____________

6 I cann see you, bat you can't see me – I'm a poltergeist. ____________ ____________

4 The fourth word

Welches Wort fehlt hier?

1 mum – mother dad – father

2 open – close push – ____________

3 he – boy she – ____________

4 new – old full – ____________

5 I – me you – ____________

5 Word snake

Sechs englische Wörter sind in der Schlange versteckt. Schreibe die deutschen Übersetzungen auf.

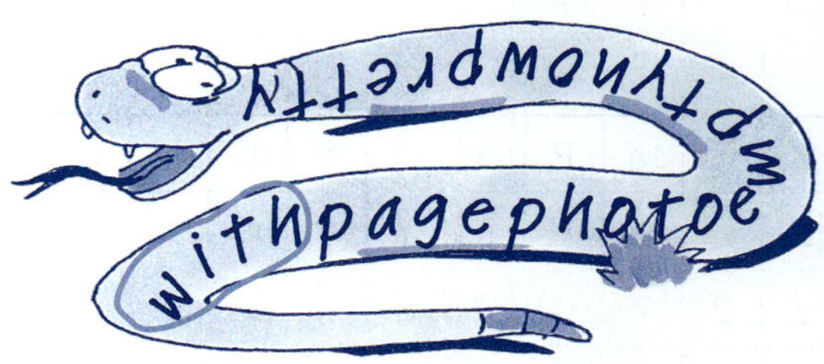

1 mit 4 ____________

2 ____________ 5 ____________

3 ____________ 6 ____________

New words ▸ p. 12

Dan und Jo leben **in der Hamiltonstraße 7**.	Dan and Jo live ______________________ .
Sie leben bei **ihrem Vater**.	They live with ______________________ .
Ihre **Mutter** heißt Catherine.	Their ____________'s name is Catherine.
Heute ist ein sehr schöner Tag.	____________ is a very nice day.
Es ist **der letzte Tag der Sommerferien**.	It's ______________________ .
Entschuldigung, dass ich zu spät komme.	______________________ .
eine **Einkaufsliste** schreiben	write a ______________________
Sehen wir uns die Liste an.	______________________ .
Du brauchst ein Lineal und zwei Bleistifte.	____________ a ruler and two pencils.
Ich brauche eine Schultasche. – **Ich auch.**	I need a school bag. – ____________
Können wir neue **Bleistiftanspitzer** haben?	Can we have new ______________________?
Und wir brauchen sechs **Schulhefte**.	And we need six ______________________ .
eine **Übung** im Wordmaster machen	do an ____________ in Wordmaster
Wir brauchen neue Filzstifte **für die Schule**.	We need new felt tips ______________________ .
Auf gehts, ihr zwei!	______________________ .
Ich **kann sagen**, was in meinem Mäppchen ist.	I ____________ what's in my pencil case.

6 Word search

Vervollständige die Einkaufsliste für die Schule.
Die fehlenden Wörter sind im Gitter versteckt. (↓ →)

W	P	N	O	Y	R	T	A	B	L
O	V	F	N	S	T	I	C	K	J
B	Y	G	U	H	R	P	Q	U	K
E	R	M	P	A	D	S	E	N	O
R	U	L	E	R	Y	P	E	N	X
Z	B	I	D	P	N	L	R	O	C
Q	B	A	G	E	W	A	V	L	A
V	E	P	E	N	C	I	L	S	S
U	R	E	X	E	R	C	I	S	E
M	R	X	V	R	P	O	F	G	U

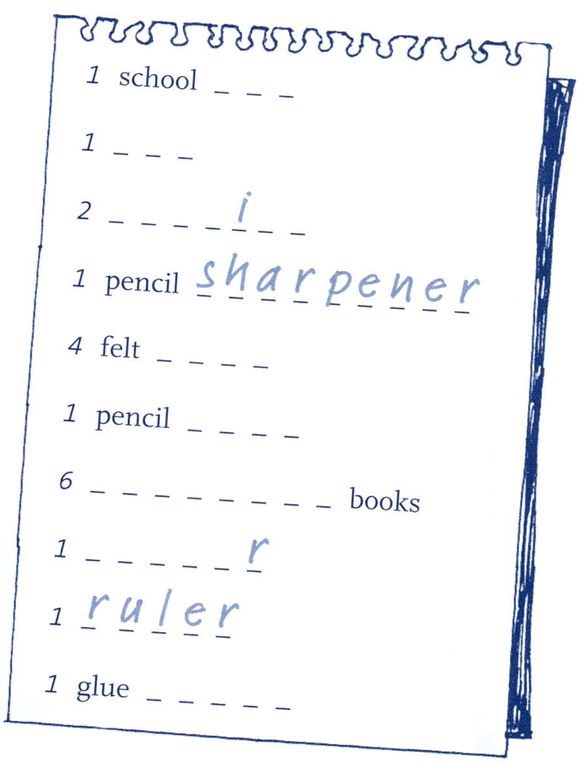

New words ▸ pp. 13 – 14

Welche Farbe hat dein Mäppchen?	______________ your pencil case?
Das ist mein grüner **Teller**.	That's my green ______________ .
Ich kann den roten Teller nicht finden. **Na gut** ...	I can't find the red plate. ______________ ...
Die Kapoors haben eine **Wohnung** in Bristol.	The Kapoors have got a ______________ in Bristol.
Sie ist **über** ihrem **Laden**.	It's ______________ their ______________ .
Nun, ist meine Schul**uniform** okay?	__________, is my school ______________ OK?
Morgen ist Montag.	______________ is Monday.
Es ist **der erste Tag an der neuen Schule**.	It's ______________ .
Hör auf damit, Dilip!	______________, Dilip!
Du kannst zum Laden gehen.	______________ .
Warum ich? Mama kann auch gehen.	______________? Mum can go too.
Ich kann ein **Gedicht** aufsagen.	I can say a ______________ .
Tag zwei der **Woche** ist Dienstag.	Day two of the ______________ is Tuesday.

7 Scrambled words

Setze die Wörter richtig zusammen und füge sie in die passende Lücke ein.

1 The Kapoors ___live___ in a ____________ over their shop. — levi, ltaf,

2 ______________________ is a big _________ for Ananda. — toormorw, yda

3 It's her ____________ day at the new ____________ . — fstri, oschol

4 Dilip, you can go to the __________ and __________ your father. — spoh, hpel

5 Why me? It's the____________ day of my ________________ too. — ltas, hodilasy

6 We __________ the newspaper ________ Cotham Park Road. — ndee, ofr

8 Words and pictures

Zeichne die folgenden Wörter.

New words ▸ pp. 15 – 16

Ich brauche eine **Zeitung** für Herrn Kapoor.	I need a ____________________ for Mr Kapoor.
Wir können jetzt **frühstücken**.	We can ____________________ now.
Was ist deine Telefonnummer?	____________________ ?
Meine Nummer ist: zwei – **null** – vier.	My number is two – _____ – four.
Ich kann die Zahlen sagen – **null**, eins, zwei ...	I can say numbers - _________, one, two ...
Können wir ein **Doppel**zimmer haben?	Can we have a ____________ room?
Prunella **kann Zauberkunststücke machen**.	Prunella ____________________ .
Willkommen in der **Frühstückspension**.	Welcome to the ____________________ .
Polly ist ein **Papagei**.	Polly is a ______________ .
Sie heißen dich in ihrem Haus **willkommen**.	____________________ their house.
Herr Hanson ist in einem **Rollstuhl**.	Mr Hanson is in a ________________ .
Herr Carter-Brown ist **bei der Arbeit**,	Mr Carter-Brown is ________________ .

9 Game corner

Löse das Zahlenrätsel und bemale das Bild mit den entsprechenden Farben.

New words ► p. 17–18

Entschuldigen Sie. Ist dies die Paulstraße?	______________ . Is this Paul Street?
Entschuldigen Sie – ich kann nicht kommen.	______________ – I can't come.
Danke! – **Bitte, gern geschehen.**	Thank you! – ______________ .
Viel Glück mit deinem neuen Drachen.	______________ with your new kite.
die **Reise zurück nach Deutschland**	the ______________

10 Bits and pieces

Setze die Bruchstücke zusammen, um Wörter zu bilden, die du gerade gelernt hast. Übersetze sie ins Deutsche.

~~o~~	ner
part	lour
pho	ther
bro	ty
emp	~~pen~~
co	to

1 open – öffnen
2 ______________
3 ______________
4 ______________
5 ______________
6 ______________

mo	come
to	paper
num	ercise
news	ber
ex	day
wel	ther

7 ______________
8 ______________
9 ______________
10 ______________
11 ______________
12 ______________

11 Odd word out

Ein Wort passt nicht. Finde und unterstreiche es.

1 purple – yellow – empty – pink
2 glue stick – holidays – pencil – ruler
3 friend – mother – father – sister
4 Monday – Tuesday – Friday – holidays
5 I – he – she – me
6 shop – wheelchair – flat – house

12 Word partners

Bilde Wortpaare.

1 mum – dad
2 apple – ______________
3 brother – ______________
4 Bristol – ______________
5 talk – ______________
6 he – ______________
7 black – ______________
8 pencil – ______________
9 England – ______________
10 today – ______________

New words ▸ pp. 18 – 19

Ich habe **viele Comic-Hefte**.	I've got ______________________ .
Es gibt eine Zeitung auf dem Stuhl.	______________ a newspaper on the chair.
Es sind zwei Bücher auf dem Tisch.	______________ two books on the table.
Wo ist die **Orangenmarmelade**?	Where's the ______________ ?
Es ist 7 Uhr **morgens**.	It's 7 o'clock ______________________ .
Was ist das englische **Wort** für „**Uhr**"?	What's the English ________ for ' ________ '?
Dies ist eine sehr hübsche **Lampe**.	This is a very nice ________ .
Das da ist deine **Milch**!	That's your ________ there!
Kann ich dein neues **Handy** sehen?	Can I see your new ______________________ ?
Wo ist mein **Geld**?	Where's my ________ ?
Das ist meine neue **Brotdose**.	That's my new ______________________ .

1 There's … / there are …

Vervollständige die Sätze mit diesen Wörtern.

Are there | there aren't | there are | there is | Is there | ~~There's~~

1 There's a photo on the table.

2 ______________ a dog in the photo?

3 Yes, ______________ .

4 ______________ parrots in the photo too?

5 No, ______________ .

6 But ______________ two cats.

2 Word snail

Übersetze die Wörter ins Englische. Trage die englischen Wörter in die Wortschnecke ein. Die Anfangsbuchstaben in der Schnecke helfen dir.

New words ▸ p. 20

Kannst du mich **vor** 8 Uhr treffen?	Can you meet me ______ eight o'clock?
Hast du **Unterricht** am Samstag?	Have you got ______ on Saturday?
Die erste **Unterrichtsstunde** ist Englisch.	The first ______ is English.
Es gibt 25 **Schüler**.	There are 25 ______ .
Sie sind sehr **aufgeregt**.	They're very ______ .
Als Erstes können wir ein Lied singen.	______ we can sing a song.
Sind die Zwillinge **klug** oder **verrückt**?	Are the twins ______ or ______ ?
Hört nicht auf Jo.	______ Jo.
Kommt und **setzt euch zu mir**!	______ and ______ .
Es ist nicht richtig – es ist **falsch**!	It's not right – it's ______ !

3 Word search

Die Buchstaben in diesen Wörtern sind durcheinandergeraten. Finde die richtigen Wörter im Gitter (↓ →).

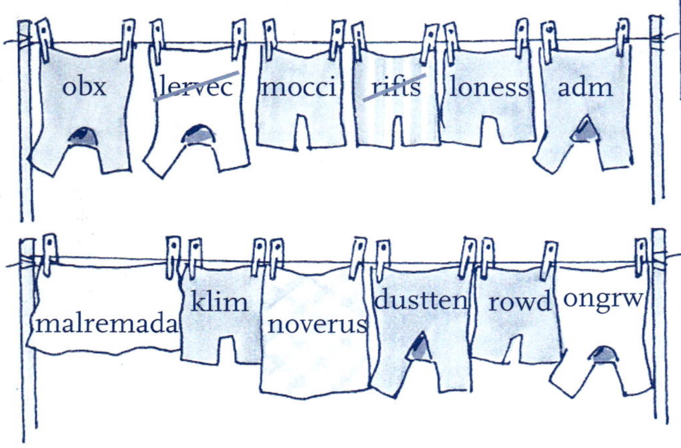

M	I	L	K	E	U	L	M	P
Q	C	O	M	I	C	Q	A	N
M	A	R	M	A	L	A	D	E
W	R	O	N	G	E	B	Y	R
O	R	T	J	T	V	O	Y	V
R	V	R	N	N	E	X	U	O
D	G	C	F	I	R	S	T	U
S	T	U	D	E	N	T	Y	S
L	E	S	S	O	N	Q	C	T

4 Word mix

Bringe die Wörter in die richtige Reihenfolge.

1 floor. the My is book on — My book is on the floor.

2 sandwich you box? got your Have ______

3 new The are school. at students the ______

4 mad Dan Are and twins? Jo the ______

5 from mum your Bristol? Is ______

New words ▸ *pp. 21 – 22*

Unsere Mutter ist aus England.	________ mum is from England.
Dies ist Ananda. **Ihr** Vater ist sehr nett.	This is Ananda. ________ dad is very nice.
Wir können **zusammen** gehen.	We can go ________________ .
Oh, **das tut mir leid.**	Oh, ________________ .
Ich komme aus Aue. – **Wie bitte**? Woher?	I'm from Aue. – ________ ? Where are you from?
Herr Kingsley ist unser Englisch**lehrer**.	Mr Kingsley is our English ________________ .
Dan und Jo sind in der **Klasse** 7PK.	Dan and Jo are in ________________ 7PK
Sagt mir eure Namen.	________________________ .
Ich mag **Sportunterricht.**	I like ________ .
Danke – ich habe **genug.**	Thank you – I've got ________________ .
Sophie ist ein **ruhiges** Mädchen.	Sophie is a ________________ girl.
Ist dies ein guter **Witz**?	Is this a good ________________ ?
Nein, er ist **schlecht.**	No, it's ________ .
Kannst du dir das merken?	________________________
Ist diese Farbe rot **oder** braun?	Is this colour red ______ brown?
Hört jetzt den **Alphabet**-Rap.	Now listen to the ________________ rap.
Wirf den **Ball**!	________________ the ________________ !
Klettere bitte nicht **auf den Baum**!	Please don't ________________________ !
Bitte **schreibe** mit dem roten Filzstift.	Please ________________ with the red felt tip.
Schau mich an und **tue, was ich tue.**	Look at me and ________________________ .
Kannst du dieses Wort **buchstabieren**?	Can you ________ this word?

5 Odd word out

Unterstreiche das Wort, das nicht passt.

1 throw – climb – enough – write

2 student – breakfast – teacher – lesson

3 I – you – bad – he

4 think – glue stick – pencil sharpener – rubber

5 nervous – quiet – mobile phone – clever

6 before – after – with – milk

7 empty – full – thing – new

8 sister – but – father – brother

New words ▸ p. 23

Dies ist euer neuer **Stundenplan**.	This is your new ______________ .
Nehmt eure Englischbücher **heraus**.	______________ your English books.
Schreibt euch meinen Namen **auf**.	______________ my name.
Dienstags ist Deutsch – **um** 9.40 Uhr.	______________ it's German – ________ 9.40.
Dann haben wir Englisch **bei** Mr Kingsley.	Then we've got English ____________ Mr Kingsley.
Nach der **Pause** habt ihr Sportunterricht.	____________ the ____________ it's PE.
Bitte geht nach dem **Mittagessen** in Raum 2.	Please go to Room 2 after ____________ .

6 Numbers and letters: School subjects

Zu jeder Zahl gehört ein Buchstabe. Finde zuerst die Lösungswörter – es sind alles Schulfächer, Dann finde den „geheimen Satz".

6 8 18 12 7 17

15 7 10 18 12 7 18

1 3 14 17 15

3 8 14

17 10 15 14 11 8 19

1 4 15 10 7

9 10 11 16 11 13 19

2 8 3 1 3

G	E	O	G	R	A	P	H	Y
13	18	11	13	8	3	5	17	19

13 18 8 1 3 12

The secret sentence

10   16 18 3 8(R) 12   18 12 13 16 10 15 17(H)   3 14(T)   15 7 17(H) 11 11 16(L) -

18 12 13 16 10 15(S) 17   16 18 15 15(S) 11 12 15   3 8 18   13 8 18(E) 3 14 !

7 Opposites

Finde die Gegenteile.

1 right – wrong

2 before – ______________

3 empty – ______________

4 pull – ______________

5 good – ______________

6 new – ______________

7 open – ______________

8 boy – ______________

New words ▸ pp. 24 – 28

Das **Essen** ist **wirklich** gut.	The ________ is ____________ good.
Ich **habe keinen** Teller.	I __________________ plate.
Er hat ein Gesicht **wie** ein **Bankräuber**!	He's got a face _______ a ____________________!
Ich brauche zwei Filzstifte – das ist **alles**.	I need two felt tips. That's _________ .
Da ist Herr Kingsley. Kannst du **ihn** sehen?	There's Mr Kingsley. Can you see _________ ?
Jack, du hast verrückte **Ideen**.	Jack, you've got mad _____________ .
Was haben wir als Nächtes?	____
Die Mathestunde war so **langweilig**.	The maths lesson was so _________________ .
Ich bin in **Klasse** 5b.	I'm in ______________ 5b.
Mädchen sind **anders als** Jungs.	Girls are _____________________________ boys.

8 Word snake: Classroom English

Finde zehn englische Wörter in der Schlange.
Setze die Wörter in die richtigen Lücken ein.

1 Can I go to the ____________?

2 Can I open the ____________?

3 Please ____________ with a partner.

4 What ____________ are we on?

5 What's for ______________?

6 Look at your worksheets please.

7 Write five ________________ please.

8 Sit at your ________________, please.

9 Don't ________________ your homework.

10 Please don't ______________!

9 What's the word: *at* or *on*?

Vervollständige die Sätze mit at *(5 x) oder* on *(3 x).*

1 We live __at__ 18 Park Street.

2 Come and see us _______ Tuesday.

3 Let's sit _______ the table there.

4 The book is _______ the table.

5 Jo and Dan are _______ school.

6 _______ 8.45 it's English with Mr Kingsley.

7 Look _______ the board, please.

8 Let's look at the pictures _______ page 24.

New words ▸ pp. 31 – 32

Es ist das **Ende** der Schule für heute.	It's the ____________ of school for today.
Beeil dich, Ananda!	______________________________ , Ananda!
Arme Sophie – sie ist sehr aufgeregt.	_______________ Sophie – she's very nervous.
Sophie und Ananda, **kommt herein**!	Sophie and Ananda, ______________________________ !
Ihr könnt mir **alles** erzählen.	You can tell me ___________________________ .
Ich mag **Tee** mit Milch.	I like _______________ with milk.
Wir haben nette **Klassenkameraden**.	We've got nice ______________________________ .
Wie **war** euer neuer Lehrer?	How ______________ your new teacher?
Deutschland, Europa, die **Welt**	Germany, Europe, the __________________
Vielen Dank Dan. **Bis bald.**	Thank you very much, Dan. _______________________ .
Nein Jack, **erzähl weiter**.	No Jack, ___________________________ .
Haben Sie **ein Päckchen Pfefferminzbonbons**?	Have you got ____________________________________ ?
Mein Freund hat eine **kleine** schwarze Katze.	My friend has got a ____________________ black cat.
Tschüs, Dan, Jo und Ananda.	________________ , Dan, Jo and Ananda.
Erzähl mir **mehr** über deine Klasse.	Tell me _______________ about your form.
Herr Kingsley **mag** Fußball.	Mr Kingsley _________________ football.
Dies ist Ananda. Ich mag **sie sehr**.	This is Ananda. I like ____________________________ .

10 Bits and pieces

Verbinde die Silben, um ein Wort zu bilden.

1	les	come	______________________
2	emp	vous	______________________
3	class	dent	______________________
4	ner	son	lesson
5	pic	mate	______________________
6	e	ture	______________________
7	stu	ty	______________________
8	wel	nough	______________________

11 The fourth word

Welches Wort fehlt hier?

1	black – white	bad – ____________________
2	he – she	his – ____________________
3	mum – dad	sister – ____________________
4	yellow – colour	five – ____________________
5	new – old	full – ____________________
6	pull – push	open – ____________________
7	I – my	we – ____________________
8	brother – father	sister – ____________________

New words ▸ p. 34

Lasst uns **einen Kalender** für Jo **machen**.	Let's ______________________ for Jo.
Er hat im Juni **Geburtstag**.	His ______________ is in June.
Wann hat Dilip Geburtstag?	__________ is Dilip's birthday?
Wir alle mögen **Weihnachten**.	We all like ______________ .
Welches **Datum** haben wir heute?	What's the __________ today?

12 Picture puzzle

Welche Wörter sind auf den Zeichnungen dargestellt? Welches ‚geheime Wort' ist im Rätsel verborgen?

1 

2 

3 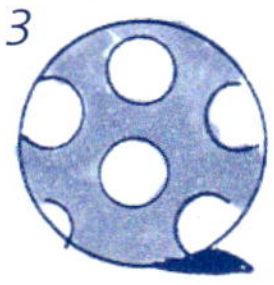

11 

5 

4 

7 

8 

6 

9 

10 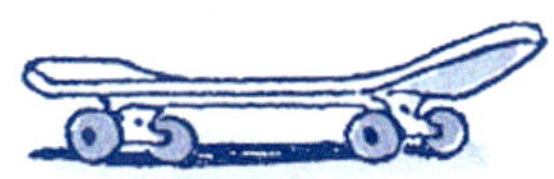

1 ___ ___ ___ ___ ___ ___ ___ ___ ___ ___ ___

2 ___ ___ ___

3 ___ ___ ___ ___

4 ___ ___ ___ ___

5 ___ ___ ___ ___ ___ ___ ___ ___

6 ___ ___ ___ ___ ___ ___

7 ___ ___ ___ ___

8 ___ ___ ___ ___ ___ ___

9 ___ ___ ___ ___ ___

10 ___ ___ ___ ___ ___ ___ ___ ___ ___ ___

11 ___ ___ ___ ___ ___ ___

13 Scrambled words: Months

Welche Monate sind das? Die markierten Buchstaben ergeben das geheime Wort.

1 beeemprst ___ ___ ___ ___ ___ ___ ___ ___ ___

2 toborec ___ ___ ___ ___ ___ ___ ___

3 ailpr ___ ___ ___ ___ ___

4 jluy ___ ___ ___ ___

5 aajnruy ___ ___ ___ ___ ___ ___ ___

14 Crossword

Across

2 German: mit / English: ★ (4)
4 German: Ausflug / English: ★ (4)
5 white – black / good – ★ (3)
9 German: Idee / English: ★ (4)
10 It's the first day at the new school. All the kids are ★. (7)
13 German: Comic-Heft / English: ★ (5)
15 German: Drachen – English: ★ (4)
17 8th July 2006 is a ★. (4)
19 My father reads a ★ every day. (9)
22 German: oder / English: ★ (2)
25 German: Rollstuhl / English: ★ (10)
26 You eat food from a ★. (5)
27 I live in a house, but my friend lives in a ★. (4)
31 German: Gedicht / English: ★ (4)
32 German: alles / English: ★ (10)
35 Things you eat. (4)
38 old – new / big – ★ (6)
40 Today is Friday and ★ is Saturday. (8)
41 The ★ break is from 12.40 to 1.40. (5)

Down

1 Write five sentences in your ★ book. (8)
2 I'm happy ★ I see my friend Ananda. (4)
3 ★ are two newspapers on the table. (5)
4 German: dann / English: ★ (4)
5 Jack, have you got your sandwich ★ ? (3)
6 His phone number is 5224: five ★ two four (6)
7 German: Foto / English: ★ (5)
8 Girl: This is her mobile phone – Boy: This is ★ mobile phone. (3)
11 German: Witz / English: ★ (4)
12 Is Jo the ★ twin? (3)
14 You can eat it on your toast. (9)
16 "I'm from Bristol." – "I'm from Bristol★." (3)
18 ★ is Monday and tomorrow is Tuesday. (5)
20 German: hübsch / English: ★ (6)
21 German: Bild / English: ★ (7)
22 I – my / we – ★ (3)
23 *3, 2, 1, 0* = three, two, one, ★ (4)
24 Are you in ★ 7PK? (4)
28 Your first ★ on Tuesday is English. (6)
29 Seven o'clock: before school / four o'clock: ★ school (5)
30 German: Uniform / English: ★ (7)
31 Open your books at ★ 24. (4)
33 This pizza is ★ good! (6)
34 It's white and you can drink it. (4)
35 The glass isn't empty – it's ★. (4)
36 The first ★ in this sentence is "The". (4)
37 This schoolbag isn't old – it's ★ (3)
39 German: Tee / English: ★ (3)

New words ▸ *pp. 36 – 37*

Schönes **Wochenende**!	Have a nice ______________________!
Sophie ist **zu Hause**.	Sophie is ____________________.
Wir haben einen schönen **Garten**.	We've got a nice __________________.
Hat Sophie ein **kleines** Zimmer?	Has Sophie got a ____________ room?
Ich **teile** mir ein Zimmer **mit** meiner Schwester.	I ____________ a room ___________ my sister.
Sechs **Leute** wohnen in unserem Haus.	Six ________________ live in our house.
Schau, es sind drei Kaninchen im **Stall**.	Look, there are three rabbits in the ____________.
Dies ist ein **Käfig** für Harry den Hamster.	This is a ____________ for Harry the hamster.
Sheeba hat einen **Korb**.	Sheeba has got a ________________.
Wir haben zwei **Wellensittiche**.	We've got two ____________________.
Und ich habe eine **Schildkröte**.	And I've got a ______________________.

1 Picture puzzle

Was sind das für komische Tiere! Welche Tiere erkennst du in den beiden Zeichnungen?

guinea pig

____

1

____

____

____

____

____

____

2

____

____

New words ▸ p. 38

Singt das Lied und **führt** es **auf**!	Sing and ________ the song!
Bitte **putz** dir deine **Zähne**, Jo.	Please ________ your ________, Jo.
Schau, Baby Hannahs erster **Zahn**!	Look, baby Hannah's first ________!
So **wasche** ich **mein Gesicht**.	This is the way I ________.
Ich gehe **früh** am Morgen in die Schule.	I go to school ________ in the morning.
Ich komme am **Nachmittag** nach Hause.	I come home in the ________?
Was sind deine **Pläne** für heute?	What are your ________ for today?
Schreibe einen **Aufsatz über** deine Familie:	Write an ________ your family:
Ein Tag im **Leben** meiner Familie	A day in the ________ of my family
Das ist doch sehr **leicht**!	That's very ________!
Ich **stehe** um 6 Uhr morgens **auf**.	I ________ at 6 o'clock in the morning.
Ich tue es **jeden** Tag.	I do it ________ day.
Warum kann ich nicht **schlafen**?	Why can't I ________?
Wasche bitte deine **Hände**.	________ your ________, please.
Da kommt mein **Bus**! Tschüs!	There's my ________! Bye!
Kann ich deinen Aufsatz **lesen**?	Can I ________ your essay?

2 Lost words

Füge das richtige Wort in die Lücken ein. Verwende die Wörter in der Wolke und im Auto.

1 I get up __at__ 6.30 __in__ the __morning__ (Morgen).

2 My cat sleeps ______ the ________________. (Nachmittag)

3 You can meet Dan ______ Friday ________________. (Abend)

4 I can see my sister ______ the ________________. (Wochenende)

5 I go to bed ______ 9.30 ______ the ________________. (Abend)

6 Dan, can you wash the car ______ Saturday

________________? (Morgen)

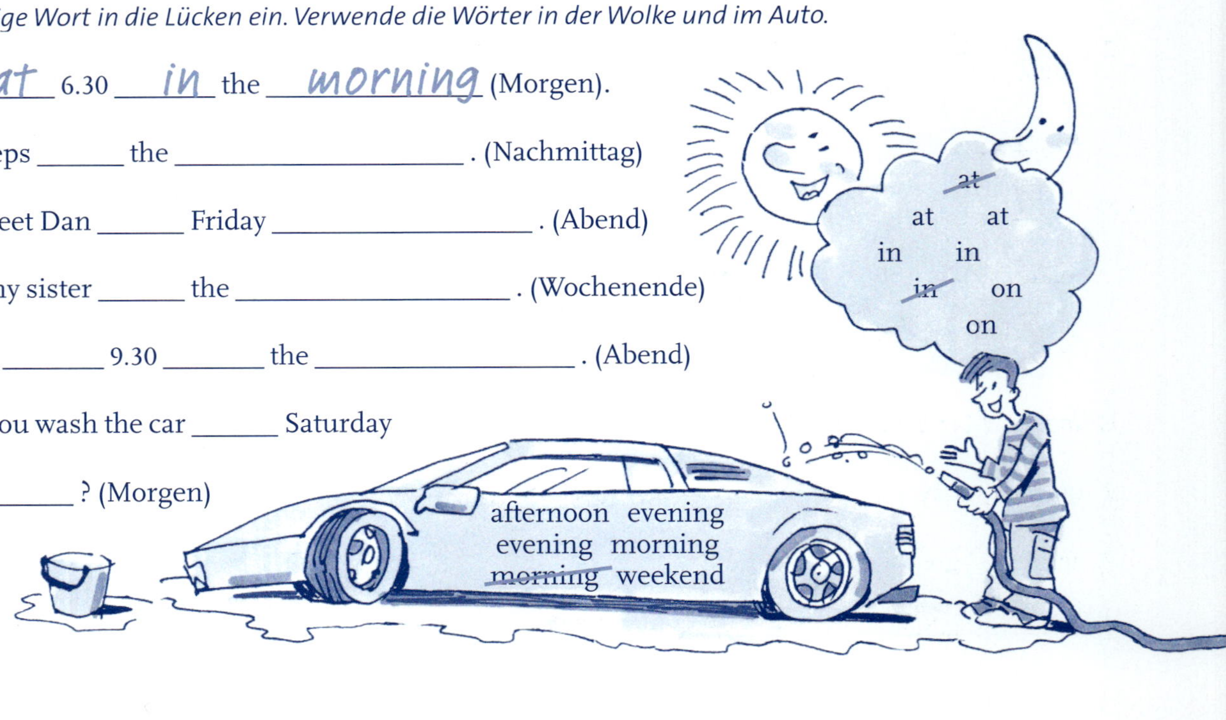

New words ► p. 39

Nach dem Frühstück **zieht** Sophie **sich an**.	After breakfast Sophie ______________________ .
Dann **gibt** sie Harry und Toby ihr Frühstück.	Then she __________ Harry and Toby their breakfast.
Sie **füttert** auch Sheeba.	She ____________ Sheeba too.
Sheeba mag **Fleisch** und **Möhren**.	Sheeba likes __________ and ________________ .
Sophie füttert die Haustiere und Toby **sieht zu**.	Sophie feeds the pets and Toby ________________ .
Können Katzen **fernsehen**?	Can cats ________________________ ?
Guck mal. Kannst du die Kaninchen **sehen**?	___________ . Can you _________ the rabbits?
Versuche das Meerschweinchen **zu** finden.	________________ find the guinea pig.
Ich **stelle** den Käfig auf den Tisch und putze ihn.	I _________ the cage on the table and clean it.
Danach füttere ich die Hamster.	__________________ I feed the hamsters.
Katzen mögen Katzen**futter**	Cats like cat ___________
... aber wir mögen indisches **Essen**!	... but we like Indian ___________ !
Wanda **trinkt** und spielt in ihrem **Goldfischglas**.	Wanda ___________ and plays in her ___________ .
Sie spielt **den ganzen Tag**.	She plays ______________ .

3 Pronunciation

Vervollständige die Listen mit Wörtern vom Zettel.
In jeder Liste müssen sich die Wörter reimen.

Markiere für jede Liste das passende Lautschriftsymbol.

do eight no ~~late~~
oh right to write

1		2		3		4	
date	əʊ	______	əʊ	kite	əʊ	go	əʊ
______	eɪ	______	eɪ	______	eɪ	______	eɪ
late	uː	too	uː	white	uː	throw	uː
plate	aɪ	two	aɪ	______	aɪ	______	aɪ

Ordne das Wort in Lautschrift dem englischen Wort zu.

1	greɪt	day	*4*	huː	food	*7*	naɪs	like	*10*	rəʊd	home
2	ˈteɪbl	great	*5*	fuːd	new	*8*	laɪk	nice	*11*	həʊm	joke
3	deɪ	table	*6*	njuː	who	*9*	raɪt	right	*12*	dʒəʊk	road

New words ▸ p. 40

Danke für deine **Hilfe.**	____________ for your ____________.
Natürlich kann ich Ihnen helfen.	____________ I can help you.
Kannst du mir das Buch geben? – **Bitte sehr!**	Can you give me the book? – ____________!
Nein, Prunella. Das ist **ganz falsch.**	No Prunella. That's ____________.
Manchmal rede ich mit Sophie.	____________ I talk to Sophie.
Aber ich **streite** nicht mit ihr.	But I don't ____________ with her.
Sophie und Prunella **machen** kein **Judo.**	Sophie and Prunella don't ____________.
Papa schaut jede **Nacht** fern – **bis** 11 Uhr !	Dad watches TV every ________ – ________ 11 o'clock!
Finde eine Zahl und einen **Buchstaben.**	Find a number and a ____________.

4 What are the words?

Vervollständige den Dialog zwischen Dan and Jo mit der richtigen Übersetzung des deutschen Wortes „bitte".

Dan Can I have a plate, ____________ (1)?

Jo ____________ (2) What do you need?

Dan A plate. P – L – A – T – E !

Jo Ah, you need a plate. ____________ (3).

Dan Thanks!

Jo ____________ (4).

5 Word search

Benutze die Silben, um acht Wörter zu bilden, die du in dieser Unit gelernt hast. Dann finde die Wörter im Gitter. (↓ →)

S	O	M	E	T	I	M	E	S
B	R	B	U	O	L	I	E	G
U	C	A	R	R	O	T	B	A
P	X	B	S	T	L	T	U	R
X	Y	A	U	O	K	U	D	D
T	I	S	W	I	B	N	G	E
S	P	K	O	S	K	B	I	N
W	E	E	K	E	N	D	E	M
A	F	T	E	R	N	O	O	N

New words ▸ *pp. 41 – 47*

Oma ist 70 und **Opa** ist 75.	______ is 70 and ______ is 75.
Schau, meine **Großeltern** und **Eltern**.	Look, my ______ and ______ .
Da – **oben** im Foto!	There – ______ the photo!
Ich mag meine Schwester, **weil** sie nett ist.	I like my sister ______ she's nice.
Oh nein! Der Hamster ist **tot**.	Oh no! The hamster is ______ .
Das **Kind** ist vier Jahre alt.	The ______ is four years old.
Die Shaws haben zwei **Kinder**.	The Shaws have got two ______ .
Wir haben auch einen **Sohn** und eine **Tochter**.	We've got a ______ and a ______ too.
Onkel Tom und **Tante** Lara leben in London.	______ Tom and ______ Lara live in London.
Catherine war **verheiratet mit** Michael.	Catherine was ______ Michael.
Dan und Jo sind unsere **Cousins**.	Dan and Jo are our ______ .
Sarah ist sechs, **also** geht sie jetzt zur Schule.	Sarah is six, ______ she goes to school now.
Wir sind die **Enkel** von Großmutter Shaw.	We're Grandma Shaw's ______ .
Ist Elizabeth **alleinstehend**?	Is Elizabeth ______ ?
Ja, sie ist **geschieden**.	Yes, she is ______ .
Gehe nicht **ohne** mich.	Don't go ______ me.
Anna ist drei – sie ist **nur** ein kleines Kind.	Anna is three – she's ______ a little child.
Kannst du dich **an** deinen Onkel **erinnern**?	Can you ______ your uncle?
Kann ich das **Ratespiel** im Fernsehen schauen?	Can I watch the ______ on TV?
Und hier sind meine **Gäste**.	And here are my ______ .

6 Word groups

Übersetze die deutschen Wörter in der Box ins Englische und füge sie in die richtige Wortgruppe ein.

school	family	pets
timetable		

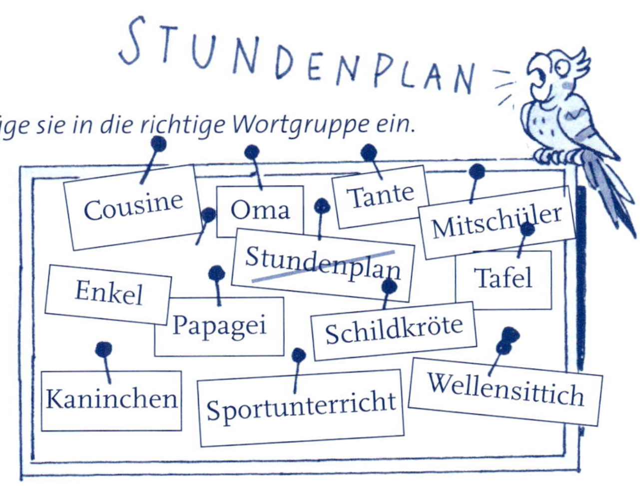

New words ▸ p. 48

Das ist ein Aufsatz **von** Daniel Shaw.	This is an essay ______ Daniel Shaw.
Zuerst **dusche** ich.	First I ______________________________ .
Jo ist unter der **Dusche**.	Jo is in the ________________ .
Wir **bereiten** unsere Sachen für die Schule **vor**.	We ________ our things ____________ for school.
Seid ihr **bereit** zu gehen?	Are you ______________ to go?
Kannst du das bitte **noch einmal** sagen?	Can you say it ______________ , please?
Ich **mache** meine **Hausaufgaben** nachmittags.	I ________ my ________________ in the afternoon.
Dieser Aufsatz ist sehr **interessant**.	This essay is very ____________________ .
Jo und drei **andere** Kinder sind hier.	Jo and three ______________ children are here.
Aus welchem **Land** kommt der **Spion**?	What ________________ is the ________ from?
Er **trägt** jeden Tag ein altes grünes T-Shirt.	He ______________ an old green T-shirt every day.
Schau, ich habe eine neue **Sonnenbrille**.	Look, I've got new ______________________ .
Wo ist meine **Brille**?	Where are my ________________ ?
Das T-Shirt ist sehr groß – es **passt** nicht.	The T-shirt is very big – it doesn't ________ .
Erzähl **uns** bitte eine **Geschichte**.	Tell ________ a ______________ , please.
Unsere Hausaufgaben sind heute **schwierig**.	Our homework is ____________________ today.
Ich denke, dieser Aufsatz ist **albern**.	I think this essay is ______________ .

7 Plurals

Trage die richtigen Pluralformen ein.

	Singular	Plural
1	day	days
2	spy	spies
3	baby	
4	essay	
5	boy	
6	family	

8 The fourth word

Welches Wort fehlt hier?

1	dog – basket	budgie – cage
2	rabbit – hutch	goldfish – ____________
3	child – children	tooth – ____________
4	good – bad	easy – ____________
5	listen – radio	watch – ____________
6	grandpa – grandma	uncle – ____________
7	early – late	single – ____________
8	1 – number	A – ____________

New words ▸ pp. 50 – 51

Erzähl mir von deinem **Traum**haus.	Tell me about your ______ house.
Ist Mutti **oben** oder **unten**?	Is mum ______ or ______ ?
Welche Farbe haben die **Treppen**?	What colour are the ______ ?
Der **Sessel** und das **Sofa** sind rot.	The ______ and the ______ are red.
Es gibt einen Fernseher im **Esszimmer**.	There's a TV in the ______ .
Der **Herd** und der **Schrank** sind neu.	The ______ and the ______ are new.
Aber die **Geschirrspülmaschine** ist sehr alt.	But the ______ is very old.
Der **Kühlschrank** ist neben der **Spüle**.	The ______ is next to the ______ .
Wir haben eine sehr große **Badewanne**.	We've got a very big ______ .
Mein Bruder hat eine tolle **Stereoanlage**.	My brother has got a great ______ .
Wie alt ist die **Waschmaschine**?	How old is the ______ ?
Ich weiß es nicht.	______ .
Besucher mögen den **Rundgang** durch das Haus.	______ like the ______ of the house.
Es **sieht** wirklich **großartig aus**.	It ______ really ______ .
Du kannst **viel** machen in diesem Haus.	You can do ______ in this house.
Schöne Dinge **passieren** die ganze Zeit.	Nice things ______ all the time.

9 Scrambled words

Prunella zeigt Uncle Henry das Haus der Carter-Browns. Setze ihre Wörter richtig zusammen. Füge sie in die passende Lücke ein.

1 In the evenings the ______ sits in the living room.	~~eeginnsv~~, afilmy
2 Mrs Carter-Brown ______ in a very comfortable green ______ .	isst, aachimrr
3 The ______ sit on the floor or on the red ______ .	cdehilnr, afos
4 The big white ______ is a ______ .	tghin, defgir
5 You can ______ ______ in the fridge. It's cold there.	ptu, dfoo
6 Do they ______ the plates in the ______ ?	swah, ikns
7 No, they put them in the ______ . ______ an hour they're clean.	dahheirssw, aefrt

10 Linking

Verbinde die Satzteile, um Fragen zu bilden. Vervollständige die Antworten.

1 Has Sheeba got	got water in her bowl?	Yes, ______
2 Is Jo	Sophie's cousins?	No, ______
3 Is Polly a	in Ananda's form?	Yes, he is.
4 Has Wanda	hamster?	No, ______
5 Are Anne and Mark	a basket in the kitchen?	Yes, ______

11 Picture crossword

Füge die richtigen Wörter ein.

Across →

Down ↓

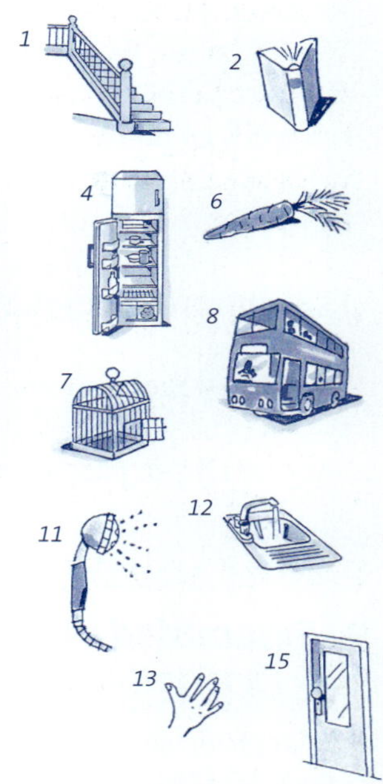

12 Word snail

Übersetze die Wörter ins Englische. Trage die englischen Wörter in die Wortschnecke ein. Die Anfangsbuchstaben in der Schnecke helfen dir.

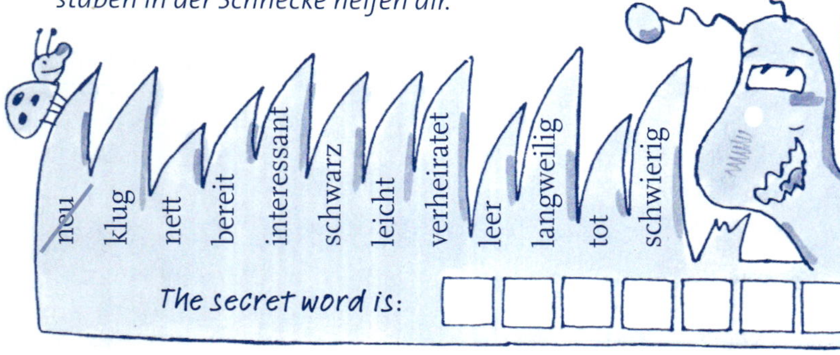

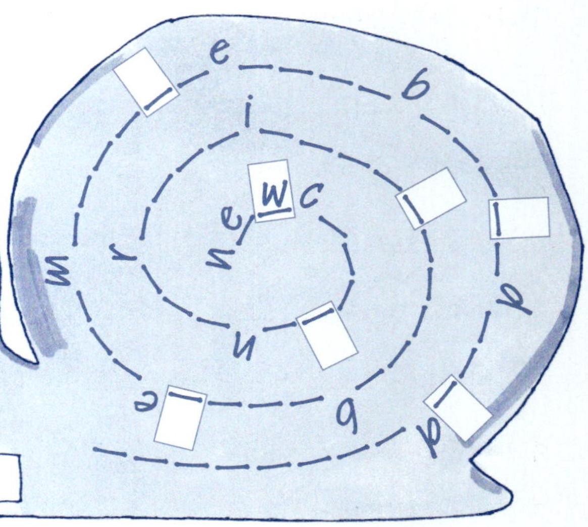

New words ▸ *pp. 52 – 53*

Papa treibt **Sport** an seinem **freien** Tag.	Dad does ____________ on his ____________ day.
Was machst du in deiner **Freizeit**?	What do you do in your ____________________ .
Martin **sammelt** alte Comics.	Martin ________________ old comics.
Ich brauche eine **Briefmarke** für diese **Karte**.	I need a ______________ for this _______________ .
Sophie **geht** jeden Sonntag **reiten**.	Sophie ________________________ every Sunday.
Toby kann nicht **Rad fahren**.	Toby can't _____________________________ .
Sophie mag ihre **Tanzstunden** sehr.	Sophie likes her __________________________ a lot.
Ich kann nicht **tanzen**.	I can't _____________ .
Ich baue **Modell**autos und spiele **Gitarre**.	I make __________ cars and play the _____________ .
Du **hast Recht** – das Buch ist sehr interessant!	You'________________ – the book is very interesting!
Ich schwimme gern. Und du?	___________________________ . What about you?

1 Scrambled words: Sports

Welche Sportarten sind das?

1 ba dminton ____ — dimnnot
2 ta____________ — beeilnnst
3 fo____________ — abllot
4 sw____________ — giimmn
5 vo____________ — abellly

2 Word partners

Verbinde die Wörter, die zusammenpassen.

go →	riding
do	volleyball
play	models
collect	the guitar
make	sport
	judo
	stamps

3 Lost words

Setze die richtigen Präpositionen ein.

1 What do you think of our poster?
2 When do you go _________ dancing lessons, Sophie?
3 Jack, look _________ photo number 5.
4 I don't like football. What _________ you, Ananda?
5 You play hockey _________ the school team, don't you?

New words ▸ p. 54

Bitte frag den **Verkäufer**.	Please ask the ______________________.
Guten Tag. Kann ich Ihnen helfen?	______________________. Can I help you?
Haben Sie dieses T-Shirt in meiner **Größe**?	Have you got this T-shirt in my ____________?
Kann ich es **anprobieren**?	Can I __________ it ______?
Diese Schuhe gefallen mir.	I like ______________ shoes.
Sie sind wirklich cool, **weißt du.**	They're really cool, ____________________.
Wissen Sie, wo ich rote Schuhe finden kann?	______ you __________ where I can find red shoes?
Diese Schuhe! Ich mag **sie** sehr!	These shoes! I like ____________ a lot!
Ich **will** auch die schwarzen Schuhe.	I ____________ the black shoes too!
Okay – **wir nehmen sie.**	OK – __________________________.
Passt mein **Oberteil**?	Does my __________ fit?

4 Word snake

Zehn englische Wörter sind in der Schlange versteckt.
Schreibe die deutschen Übersetzungen auf.

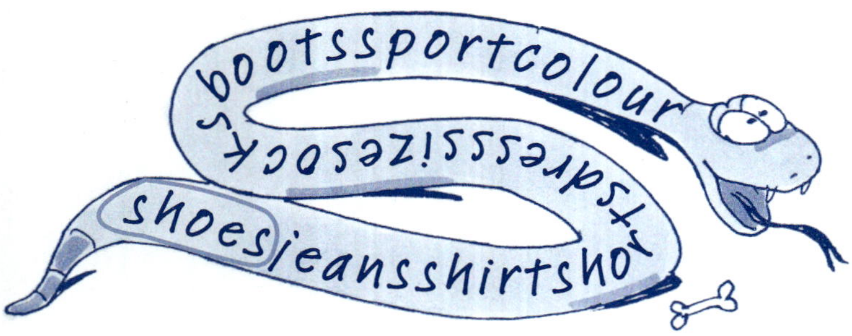

1 Schuhe
2 ______
3 ______
4 ______
5 ______
6 ______
7 ______
8 ______
9 ______
10 ______

5 Spot the mistakes

In jedem Satz gibt es zwei Fehler. Unterstreiche und korrigiere sie.

1 Can yu help me? We need hockey shoes for my doghter. you ______ ______
2 Dos this hockey schu fit, Ananda? ______ ______
3 Ananda, do you laik the calour? ______ ______
4 They look verry nice. Can I trei them on? ______ ______
5 Mum, I wont these red and wheit shoes. ______ ______
6 Yu like them, so we'll teek them. ______ ______

New words ▸ *p. 55*

Lass uns ein **Projekt über** Hobbys machen.	Let's do a ______________________ hobbies.
Du kannst Jack **fragen**.	You can ____________ Jack.
Kann er **Klavier** spielen?	Can he play ______________________?
Spielst du **allein** Tennis, Prunella?	Do you play tennis ______________, Prunella?
Kims Hund hat einen schwarz-weißen **Kopf**.	Kim's dog has got a black and white ____________.
Prunella singt **immer** in diesem Zimmer.	Prunella ______________ sings in this room.
Glaubst du, wir können **gewinnen**?	Do you think we can ____________?
Unsere **Nachbarn** reden nicht mit uns.	Our ______________________ don't talk to us.
Aber wir mögen sie **sowieso** nicht!	But we don't like them ______________!

6 Word search

Finde im Gitter weitere Wörter, die du bisher in Unit 3 gelernt hast (↓ →).

V	M	A	S	I	Z	E	G	B	X
Z	P	S	U	L	L	P	N	T	U
A	R	K	R	D	W	I	N	X	S
L	O	Y	W	H	E	A	D	E	T
O	J	G	B	W	A	N	T	F	A
N	E	I	G	H	B	O	U	R	M
E	C	V	D	R	E	D	Z	E	P
Q	T	O	P	X	X	Y	O	E	W

1 size ______________ 7 ______________

2 ______________ 8 ______________

3 ______________ 9 ______________

4 ______________ 10 ______________

5 ______________ 11 ______________

6 ______________ 12 ______________

7 Picture puzzle

Finde acht weitere Dinge.

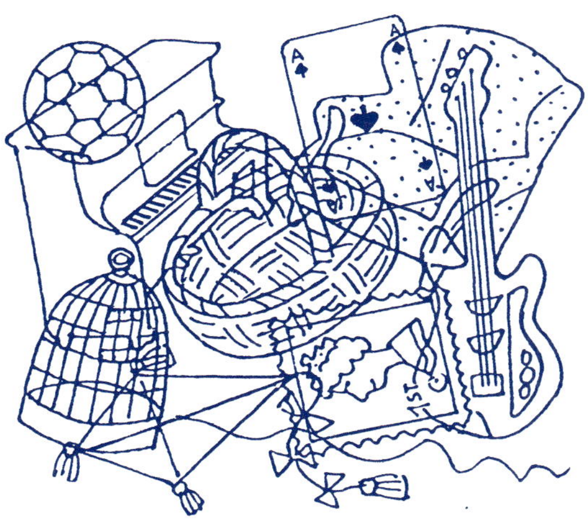

1 guitar ______________

2 ______________

3 ______________

4 ______________

5 ______________

6 ______________

7 ______________

8 ______________

9 ______________

New words ▸ p. 56

Kim schreibt **oft** E-Mails.	Kim ______ writes e-mails.
Lieber Tim, dies ist nur eine **schnelle** E-Mail.	______ Tim, this is just a ______ e-mail.
Ich habe **einige Fragen** für dich.	I've got ______ for you.
Du **stellst** auch viele **Fragen**!	You ______ lots of ______ too!
Kannst du heute oder morgen **antworten**?	Can you ______ today or tomorrow?
Und hier ist die **Antwort auf** deine Frage:	And here's the ______ your question:
Ich gehe oft zu Fußball**spielen**.	I often go to football ______.
Liebe Grüße, Kim.	______, Kim
Am nächsten Tag findet Kim eine Antwort:	______ Kim finds an answer:
Ich gehe **nie** zu Hockeyspielen.	I ______ go to hockey matches.
Ich mache **normalerweise** keinen Sport.	I don't ______ do sport.
Aber ich **gehe** immer **zu Fuß** in die Schule.	But I always ______ to school.
Grüß deine Mutter **von mir**.	______ your mum ______.

8 Numbers and letters

Zu jeder Zahl gehört genau ein Buchstabe. Finde zuerst die Lösungswörter und dann den „geheimen Satz".

1 I play tennis at ___ ___ ___ ___ ___ (3 16 17 4 13) when you're all in ___ ___ ___ (5 21 11).

2 Uncle Henry hasn't got a ___ E ___ ___ (4 21 10 11), so I ___ ___ ___ ___ ___ ___ (10 1 6 10 14 20) win.

3 I never go to football ___ ___ ___ ___ ___ ___ ___ (9 10 13 18 4 21 20) – they're ___ ___ ___ ___ ___ ___ (5 7 8 16 3 17).

4 Can you A N S W E R (10 3 20 6 21 8) a question for me?

5 Have you got a ___ ___ ___ ___ (5 16 12 21)? How ___ ___ ___ ___ ___ (7 15 13 21 3) do you ride it?

The secret sentence

___ (16) ___ ___ ___ ___ (11 7 3 13) ___ ___ ___ ___ ___ ___ (8 21 10 1 1 14) ___ ___ ___ ___ (1 16 12 21) ___ ___ (9 14) ___ ___ ___ (3 21 6)

___ ___ ___ ___ ___ ___ (13 21 3 3 16 20) ___ ___ ___ ___ ___ (20 4 7 21 20).

New words ▸ p. 57

Jack **hasst** Sport.	Jack ________________ sport.
Jetzt **muss** er seine Hausaufgaben machen.	Now he ________________ do his homework.
Zumindest muss er nicht Tennis spielen.	________________ he doesn't have to play tennis.
Die meisten Menschen mögen Haustiere.	________________ like pets.
Ich **verstehe** viele englische Wörter.	I ________________ lots of English words.
Bitte **decke den Tisch** für das **Abendessen**.	Please ________________ for ____________ .
Mach das bitte **jetzt sofort**.	Please do it ________________ .
Herr Brown **unterrichtet** in unserer Schule.	Mr Brown ________________ at our school.
Benutze den Wordmaster, um Wörter zu **lernen**.	Use Wordmaster to ________________ words.

9 Word mix

Bringe die Satzteile in die richtige Reihenfolge.

1 in their free time? / most people do / What do

What do most people do in their free time?

2 plays basketball. / Jack's dad / OnWednesdays

____

3 or do yoga. / play basketball / Jack doesn't

____

4 I have to / for dinner. / lay the table

____

5 dad have to / Why does / play basketball?

____

10 Odd word out

Finde und unterstreiche das Wort, das nicht passt.

1 football – hockey – swimming – music

2 always – never – shop assistant – sometimes

3 friend – fit – neighbour – uncle

4 breakfast – dinner – hobby – lunch

5 ask – learn – size – understand

6 shout – sing – talk – walk

New words ▸ *pp. 58 – 64*

Zeichne eine Wort**schlange** für deinen Partner.	Draw a word ______________ for your partner.
Kennst du wirklich alle neuen Namen?	Do you really ______________ all the new names?
Kann ich jetzt einen **Termin** machen?	Can I make an ______________ now?
Treffen wir uns um 9 Uhr – **unter** dem Baum!	Let's __________ at 9 o'clock – __________ the tree!
Ist dieser **Satz** richtig?	Is this ______________ right?
Dürfen wir im Park **Inliner fahren**?	Can we ______________ in the park?
Hat Ananda neue **Inliner**?	Has Ananda got new ______________ ?
Ich höre oft Musik **im Radio**.	I often listen to music ______________ .
Was ist das **Gegenteil** von „weiß"?	What's the ______________ of 'white'?
Kannst du das Wort mit einem Bild **verbinden**?	Can you ______________ the word with a picture?
Heute muss Emily das **Auto** waschen.	Today Emily has to wash the ______________ .
Bitte lies **Teil** 2 noch einmal.	Please read ______________ 2 again.

11 Pronunciation

Finde das Wort in jeder Gruppe, das wegen der Aussprache nicht passt.

1 packet – May – page packet

2 band – happen – take ______________

3 plan – name – mad ______________

4 eight – day – that ______________

5 make – bank – match ______________

6 baby – dad – play ______________

12 Word web

Finde Wörter, die in das Spinnennetz passen. Alle Wörter haben vier Buchstaben und enden auf –e.

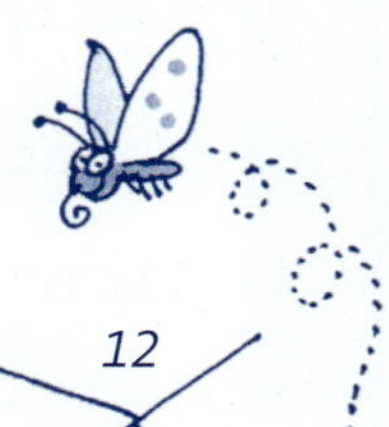

1 It flies, but it's not a bird.
2 Open your book at ★ 10.
3 Your school uniform is very ★, Ananda.
4 It's the opposite of 'there'.
5 Tell me ★ about your new class.
6 October 3rd is an important ★.
7 Today we can come ★ late.
8 Harry the hamster lives in a ★.
9 Wash your ★, Jack.
10 We ★ in Bristol.
11 You wear it on of your feet.
12 Ananda needs a ★ four hockey shoe.
13 Prunella, what do you do in your ★ time?
14 There are ★ apples for you in the kitchen.

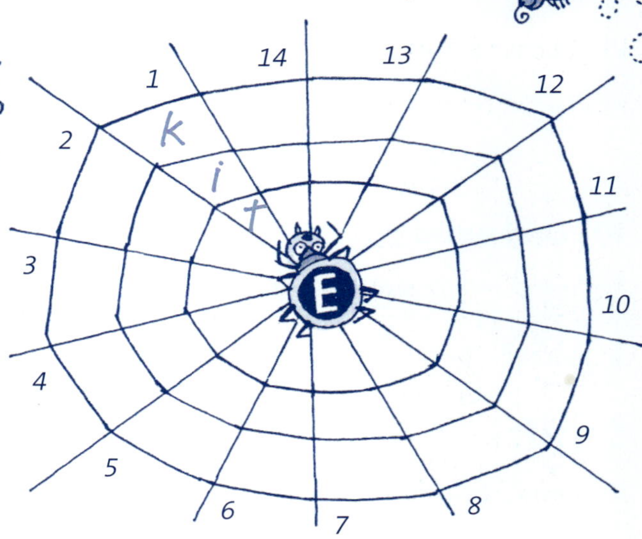

New words ▸ *pp. 65 – 66*

Ich kann zwei **Männer** und eine **Frau** sehen.	I can see two ________ and a ____________ .
Nein, es sind zwei **Frauen** und ein **Mann**!	No, there are two ____________ and one ________ !
Sie sind **die einzigen** Menschen hier.	They're ____________________ people here.
Plötzlich hört Jo ein **Geräusch**.	____________________ Jo hears a ____________ .
Vor dem Zimmer steht ein **unheimlicher** Mann.	________________ the room is a ____________ man.
Jo **rennt aus** dem Haus	Jo _________________________ the house
... und **in** den Garten.	... and ___________ the garden.
Kannst du mich morgen **anrufen**?	Can you _____________ me tomorrow?
Das ist Christina, aber wir **nennen** sie Tina.	This is Christina, but we __________ her Tina.
Wo **ist** die **Polizei**?	Where ________ the ______________ ?
Vielleicht brauchen wir ihre Hilfe.	_________________ we need their help.
Es geht um den unheimlichen Mann.	______________________ the scary man.
Wir müssen mehr über ihn **herausfinden**.	We have to ____________________ more about him.
Wir sind gute **Detektive**.	We are good _____________________ .
Du kannst auf dieses **Stück Papier** schreiben.	You can write on this _________________________ .
Du musst nur einen Buchstaben **ergänzen**.	You only have to __________ one letter.
Sie **fangen** immer um 7 Uhr mit der Arbeit **an**.	They always _______________ work at 7 o'clock.
Tina hat eine neue **Armbanduhr**.	Tina has got a new ______________ .
Jo **plant**, Herrn Green zu beobachten.	Jo ____________ to watch Mr Green.

13 Word friends

Welche Wörter passen zu dem, was die Maus denkt? Finde für jede Maus die zwei richtigen Käsestücke.

New words ▸ p. 67

Gehen wir zum **Wohltätigkeitsbasar**!	Let's go to the ____________________ !
Ich habe zehn **Pfund**.	I've got ten ____________ .
Und Sue hat ein Pfund und fünf **Pence**.	And Sue has got one pound and five ________ .
Es liegt ein **Penny** unter dem Sofa.	There's a ___________ under the sofa.
In England hat man Pfund und nicht **Euro**.	In England they've got pounds, not _________ .
Ein Euro hat 100 **Cent**.	There are 100 _________ in one euro.
Wie wär's mit 7 Pfund für diese CD?	_________________ £ 7.00 for this CD?
Das ist **zu viel** für mich.	That's _____________ for me.
Was kostet dieses Bild?	____________________ this picture?
Es kostet 2 Pfund 30.	______ £ 2.30.
Dieses Mäppchen kostet **nur** 50 Pence.	This pencil case is _________ 50 pence.
Kannst du 10 Pence **abziehen**?	Can you _________ 10 pence ______ ?
Kannst du mir bitte das **Wechselgeld** geben?	Can you give me the ____________ , please?

14 Crossword

Across →

2 These shoes don't fit. I need ★ four. (4)
3 Don't ★ – I can hear you. (5)
5 Dan and Jo are the ★ twins in their class. (4)
6 man – men/ woman – ★ (5)
8 Sherlock Holmes is a famous ★. (9)
10 Opposite of always (5)
12 Black is the ★ of white. (8)
15 ★ me tomorrow. Here's my number. (4)
16 Uncle Henry hasn't got a ★. (4)
18 Students always have to ★ things. (5)
19 pound – penny/ euro – ★ (4)

Down ↓

1 100 pence = 1 ★ (5)
2 Tennis is my favourite ★. (5)
4 he – him/they – ★ (4)
7 I haven't got enough ★ for new shoes. (5)
9 Great Britain – pound/ Germany – ★ (4)
11 Opposite of hate (4)
13 There's the bank robber. We have to call the ★. (6)
14 In his ★ time my father collects stamps. (4)
15 We've got a new ★. We always wash it on Saturday. (3)
16 Opposite of like (4)
17 ★ 5 to 11 and you've got 16. (3)

New words ▸ *pp. 68 – 69*

Kim **isst** immer Toast **zum** Frühstück.	Kim always __________ toast __________ breakfast.
Ich mag Hühnchen und **Pommes frites**.	I like chicken and ________________ .
Kann ich einige **Kekse** haben?	Can I have some ________________________ ?
Tut mir Leid. Wir haben nur **Kartoffelchips**.	Sorry. We've only got ___________________ .
Der **Obstsalat** steht auf dem Tisch.	The __________________________ is on the table.
Isst du **Würstchen** zum Frühstück?	Do you have _______________________ for breakfast?
Magst du englische **Süßigkeiten**?	Do you like English ____________________ ?
Ist der Tee **süß** genug?	Is the tea ________________ enough?
Kauft bitte drei **Flaschen Milch**.	Please buy three ______________________________ .
Kannst du bitte das **Glas** waschen?	Can you wash the ________________, please.
Der Orangensaft ist im großen **Krug**.	The orange juice is in the big ___________ .
Möchtest du ein Glas Saft?	______________________________ a glass of juice?
Und Kuchen? **Möchtest du etwas**?	And cake? ____________________________________ ?
Ja, **ich hätte gerne** etwas Saft und Kuchen.	Yes, _________________ some juice and cake.

1 Word search

Wo sind alle diese leckeren Sachen in dem Gitter versteckt?
Suche dieses Mal in drei Richtungen. (↓ → ↘)

H	A	M	B	U	R	G	E	R
S	P	I	Z	Z	A	N	R	C
C	A	P	P	L	E	C	P	U
H	R	U	X	T	W	H	O	K
I	B	I	S	C	U	I	T	S
P	F	Y	S	A	X	C	A	C
S	Y	S	W	P	G	K	T	A
J	C	H	E	E	S	E	O	K
B	R	E	A	D	Z	N	R	E

New words ▸ p. 70

Schau – eine **Einladung zu** Sophies Party!	Look – an ____________ Sophie's party!
Kann sie alle ihre Freunde **einladen**?	Can she ____________ all her friends?
Dies ist aber eine **lange** Liste.	But this is a ____________ list.
Nein, sie ist **kurz**.	No, it's ____________ .
Willst du Kim und Simon einladen?	Do you ____________ invite Kim and Simon?
Ja, natürlich. Ich mag sie **beide**.	Yes, of course. I like them ____________ .
Sie sind **echte** Freunde.	They're ____________ friends.

2 What are the words?

Was ist hier dargestellt? Die Wörter in der Imbissbude helfen dir.

1  a plate of chips

2  ____________

3  ____________

4  ____________

5  ____________

6  ____________

3 Odd word out

Finde und unterstreiche das Wort, das nicht passt.

1 cake – euro – hamburger – bread
2 pound – penny – glass – cent
3 biscuit – fruit salad – sweets – milk
4 ball – dancing – table tennis – judo
5 boots – shoes – socks – top
6 children – women – men – grandchild

4 Opposites

Finde die Gegenteile.

1 short long
2 late ____________
3 downstairs ____________
4 with ____________
5 close ____________
6 night ____________

New words ► p. 71

Ich brauche **immer noch** ein **Geschenk**.	I ______________ need a ______________________ .
Was kann ich für Sophie **kaufen**?	What can I ___________ for Sophie?
Vielleicht **Seife** – oder ein **witziges** Buch?	Maybe _____________ or a _______________ book?
Bücher sind nicht zu **teuer**.	Books aren't too ________________________ .
Hast du **irgendwelche** Ideen, Ananda?	Have you got ___________ ideas, Ananda?
Wie wär's mit **Ohrringen**?	What about ______________________ ?
Und Sophie hat **keine** witzigen Socken.	And Sophie has'_____ got ___________ funny socks.
Beeil dich – wir müssen Jack helfen.	______________________ – we have to help Jack.
Warum **hast du** es immer **eilig**?	Why ______________ always ______________________ ?
Wir müssen Herrn Green **verfolgen**.	We have to __________________ Mr Green.
Schreibt euch einige **Stichworte** auf.	Write down some ________________________ .
Ich habe **eine andere** Idee.	I've got _____________________ idea.

5 Word snail

Übersetze die Wörter ins Englische. Trage die englischen Wörter in die Wortschnecke ein. Die Anfangsbuchstaben in der Schnecke helfen dir.

6 Spot the mistakes

In jedem Satz gibt es zwei Fehler. Unterstreiche und korrigiere sie.

1 We still has to buy a present for Sophies birthday. have ______________ ______________

2 We doesn't know what CDs Sophie have got. ______________ ______________

3 Sophie like to read and she has got lots of book. ______________ ______________

7 Word groups

Übersetze die Wörter ins Englische. Schreibe die englischen Wörter an die passende Stelle.

1

3

4

1: bath ____

3: essay ____

4: meat ____

2

brother ____

~~Aufsatz~~	Mutter
~~Badewanne~~	Oberteil
~~Bruder~~	Obst
Cousine	Onkel
Eltern	Opa
~~Fleisch~~	Orangenmarmelade
Geschirrspüler	Pause
~~Hemd~~	Radiergummi
Hühnchen	Schlafzimmer
Kartoffeln	Schokolade
Käse	Schrank
Kekse	Schuhe
Klassenkameradin	Schüler
Klebestift	Schulheft
Kleid	Sessel
Kuchen	Shorts
Küche	Sofa
Kühlschrank	Sportunterricht
Lehrer	Spülbecken
Limonade	Stiefel
Lineal	Sweatshirt
Mäppchen	Unterrichtsstunde

5

shirt ____

New words ▸ p. 72

Sophie **macht sich für** die Party **fertig**.	Sophie ______________________ the party.
Sie **räumt** jetzt ihr Zimmer **auf**.	She' __________________ her room now.
Prunella, du **bringst alles durcheinander**.	Prunella, you' ________________________ .
Leg bitte diese Bücher **weg**.	Please put these books __________ .
Kannst du den Käfig in die Küche **bringen**?	Can you __________ the cage to the kitchen?
Emily geht **hinauf** in ihr Zimmer.	Emily is going ______ to her room.
Jetzt rennt sie wieder **hinunter**!	Now she's running __________ again!
Sie will jetzt **zu Jenny** gehen.	She wants to go __________________ now.
Sie darf **später** gehen, aber nicht jetzt!	She can go ______________ , but not now!

8 Lost words

Finde die fehlenden Wörter.

1 I always have cornflakes __for__ breakfast. What __________ you?

2 Emily is going up ______ her room.

3 Are we ready _______ the party?

4 Sophie has got lots ______ books.

5 Sophie's mum is ______ the kitchen.

6 Please put the sandwiches ______ the table, Emily.

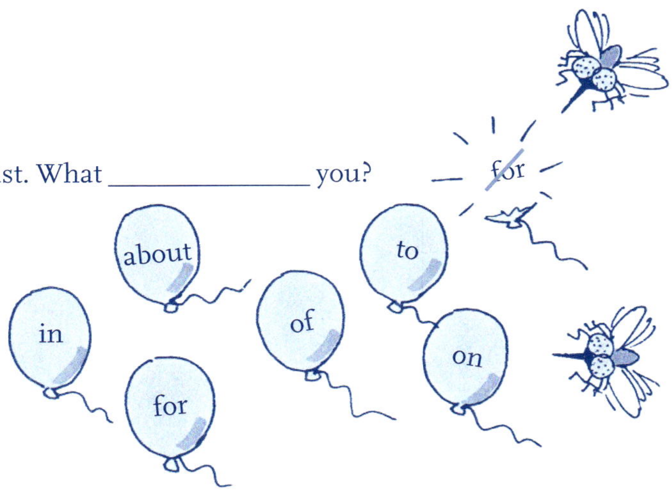

9 An English-German crossword

Across

~~3~~ (to) ask (6)
4 crisps (5)
6 (to) teach (6)
8 funny (6)
10 soap (5)
13 jug (4)
14 earring (7)
18 key word (9)
19 biscuit (4)
20 invitation (9)
21 never (3)

Down

1 really (8)
2 short (4)
3 (to) follow (6)
5 anyway (7)
7 present (8)
9 expensive (5)
11 sausage (5)
12 milk (5)
15 (to) hate (6)
16 (to) win (8)
17 these (5)

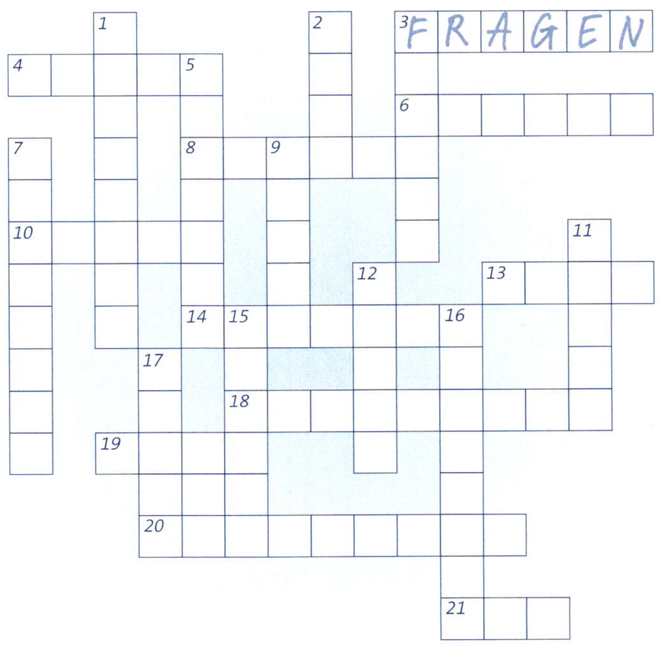

New words ▸ p. 73

Ananda, bist du **am Bahnhof**?	Ananda, are you ______ the ______________?
Ich bin **vor** der Tierhandlung.	I'm ______________________ the petshop.
Kannst du mich **hören**?	Can you ____________ me?
Schau, Herr Green ist **im Zug**.	Look, Mr Green is _______ the _____________ .
Ich **warte** gerade **auf** ihn.	I' __________________________ him.
Jetzt kommt **jemand**!	__________________ is coming now!
Steige am nächsten Bahnhof **aus**.	_________________ at the next station.
Und wo **steige** ich in den Bus **ein**?	And where do I ______________ the bus?
Ich habe ein **Paket** für dich.	I've got a __________________ for you.
Sieh dich um – es liegt auf dem Tisch.	_________________________ – it's on the table.
Du kannst das Geld hier **verstecken**.	You can ____________ the money here.
Welches Brötchen hättest du gerne?	___________________________ would you like?

10 What's this?

Schau dir Willy den Außerirdischen an und beschrifte die Körperteile.

1 hair

2 ____________

3 ____________

4 ____________

5 ____________

6 ____________

7 ____________

8 ____________

9 ____________

10 ____________

11 ____________

12 ____________

13 ____________

14 ____________

New words ▸ pp. 81 – 82

Kennst du dieses **Theaterstück**?	Do you know this ______________?
Ich mag alle vier **Szenen**.	I like all four ______________.
Es beginnt um 11 Uhr **abends**.	It starts at eleven ________.
Nein, es beginnt um 11 Uhr **vormittags**!	No, it starts at eleven ________!
Mach dir keine Sorgen, Jo.	______________, Jo.
Ich **mache mir** immer **Sorgen** um Dan.	I always ______________ Dan.
Er ist 45 **Minuten** zu spät.	He's 45 ______________ late.
Kannst du die **Türklingel** hören?	Can you hear the ______________?
Herr Shaw öffnet die **Tür**.	Mr Shaw is opening the ______________.
Wer ist an der **Haustür**?	Who is at the ______________?
Lass uns **drinnen** spielen.	Let's play ______________.
Es ist zu heiß **draußen**.	It's too hot ______________.
Diese Kekse sind **fantastisch**.	These biscuits are ______________.
Ja, aber sie sind **so** teuer.	Yes, but they're ________ expensive.
Sophie **hat** keine **Angst vor** Prunella.	Sophie ________ not ______________ Prunella.
Kannst du mir bitte den Tee **herüber reichen**?	Can you ______________ me the tea, please?
Und bitte **gib** die Chips **herum**.	And please ______________ the crisps.
Es gibt **keine** Würstchen **mehr**.	There are ______________ sausages.
Und es gibt **keine** Äpfel auf dem Tisch.	And there are ________ apples on the table.
Schreib bitte eine kurze **Mitteilung** an Klaus.	Write a short ______________ to Klaus, please.
Bitte **macht euch Notizen**.	Please ______________.
Sucht euch auch einen neuen Partner **aus**.	______________ a new partner too.
Du kannst einen **Preis** gewinnen.	You can win a ______________.
Die Partyspiele **sind** jetzt **vorüber**.	The party games ______________ now.
Sophie, **wovon redest du**?	Sophie, ______________?
Wie können wir zum Bahnhof **kommen**?	How can we ______________ to the station?
Was ist der **Titel** unseres Theaterstücks?	What's the ______________ of our play?

11 Word partners

Suche den geeigneten Wortpartner aus dem Tausendfüßler und übersetze das neue Wort ins Deutsche.

1 arm + chair = armchair – Sessel

2 basket + ______ = ______ – ______

3 bath + ______ = ______ – ______

4 class + ______ = ______ – ______

5 door + ______ = ______ – ______

6 down + ______ = ______ – ______

7 every + ______ = ______ – ______

8 foot + ______ = ______ – ______

9 home + ______ = ______ – ______

10 week + ______ = ______ – ______

12 Scrambled words

Welches Wort ist gesucht? Die Buchstabenrätsel im Leuchtturm helfen dir.

1 Would you like a ★ of water? _ _ _ _ _

2 Listen, can you ★ the dogs in the park? _ _ _ _

3 There's ★ present for Sophie. _ _ _ _ _ _ _

4 Dan, can you open the ★, please? _ _ _ _

5 Go ★ Prunella. I have to do my homework. _ _ _ _

6 Let's buy some ★ for Sophie. _ _ _ _ _ _ _ _

7 A woman is giving Mr Green a ★. _ _ _ _ _ _

8 I like chicken and ★ very much. _ _ _ _ _

9 The first ★ is a really cool pen. _ _ _ _ _

10 Listen! The ★ is playing again. _ _ _ _ _

The secret word is _ _ _ _ _ _ _ _ _ _

New words ▸ *pp. 84 – 85*

Diese Unterrichtsstunde **endet** um 9 Uhr.	This lesson ______________ at 9 o'clock.
Bitte schaut auf das **schwarze Brett**.	Please look at the ______________________________ .
Schauen wir uns das **Programm** an.	Let's look at the ______________________________ .
Lasst uns die Stühle grün **anmalen**.	Let's __________________ the chairs green.
Auf dem Poster ist ein **Schiff**.	There's a ________________ on the poster.
Möchtest du bei der **Probe** zusehen?	Would you like to see the ______________________ ?
Wir **proben** gerade die dritte Szene.	We'_____________________________ the third scene.
Ich mag den **Frühling** sehr.	I like __________________ a lot.
Der **Herbst** und der **Winter** sind auch schön.	________________ and ________________ are nice too.
Es war eine großartige **Show**.	It was a great ________________ .
Kannst du mir deine neuen CDs **zeigen**?	Can you _________________ me your new CDs?
Können wir Handys in die Schule **mitbringen**?	Can we _________________ mobile phones to school?
Und wann können wir sie **benutzen**?	And when can we ______________ them?
Was ist das **Ergebnis** des Hockeyspiels?	What's the __________________ of the hockey match?
Unser **Junioren**tanzklub ist sehr gut.	Our __________________ dance club is very good.
Kannst du den **Chor** hören?	Can you hear the _________________ ?
Sie **üben** gerade ein **Piraten**lied.	They'_____________________ a _______________ song.
Alles ist sehr **aufregend**.	Everything is very _______________________ .

1 Odd word out

Unterstreiche das Wort, das hier nicht passt.

1 summer – autumn – night – winter

2 sing – draw – paint – write

3 sometimes – today – often – always

4 tortoise – snake – hutch – guinea pig

5 football – baseball – tennis – dancing

2 The fourth word

Welches Wort wird hier gesucht?

1 cent – euro / penny – pound

2 invite – invitation / rehearse – _______________

3 see – eye / hear – _______________

4 black – white / up – _______________

5 sausage – food / lemonade – _______________

New words ▸ p. 86

Wo **warst** du letzten Freitag?	Where ______ you last Friday?
Frau Black ist verheiratet; **Frau** White ist ledig.	Mrs Black is married; ______ White is single.
Schau, Sophie spricht gerade mit ihrer **Gruppe**.	Look, Sophie is talking to her ______ .
Deine Idee **hört sich** sehr gut **an**.	Your idea ______ very good.
Ich mag den **Klang** deiner Gitarre.	I like the ______ of your guitar.
Die **Kinder** möchten die Show sehen.	The ______ would like to see the show.
Wie viel kosten vier **Eintrittskarten**?	How much are four ______ ?
Gestern war ich im **Kino**.	______ I was at the ______ .
Lass uns heute ins **Schwimmbad** gehen.	Let's go to the ______ today.
Nein – ich will ins **Sportzentrum**.	No – I want to go the ______ .

3 Word web

Trage die englische Übersetzung dieser Wörter in das Spinnennetz ein. Alle englischen Wörter enden auf -r.

~~1~~ Wasser
~~2~~ Farbe
3 Papier
4 Antwort
5 Abendessen
6 später
7 Winter
8 Jugend-
9 Chor
10 Nummer
11 Stuhl
12 Gitarre
13 Finger
14 Schwester

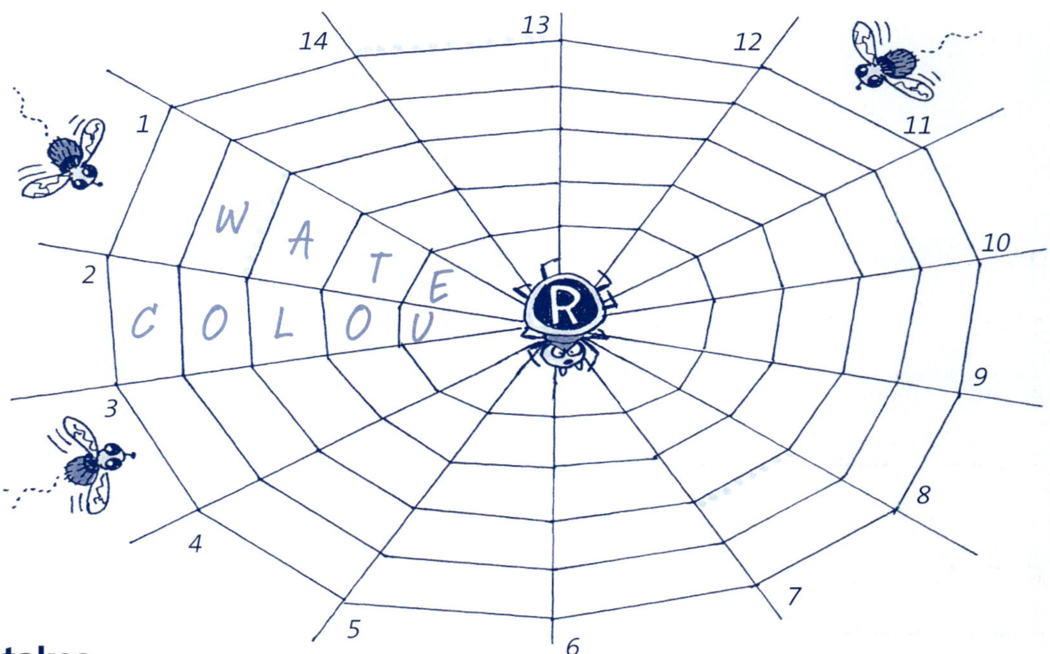

4 Spot the mistakes

In jedem Satz sind zwei Fehler. Unterstreiche und korrigiere sie.

1 The choir was very <u>gud</u> jesterday. good ______ ______

2 The childrens are rehearsing vor the show. ______ ______

3 Tell us more about the programm – it saunds great. ______ ______

4 We can't waite too see the show. ______ ______

New words ▸ p. 87

Das war ein **schrecklicher** Film.	That was a ______________ film.
Wir alle machen **Fehler**.	We all make ______________ .
Ich kann es kaum erwarten, dich zu sehen.	______________ to see you.
Vor zehn Minuten war Jack hier.	Jack was here ten minutes ______________ .
Kannst du mich um 9 Uhr **anrufen**?	Can you ______________ me at 9 o'clock?
Kann ich dein **Telefon** benutzen?	Can I use your ______________ ?

5 Pronunciation

Vervollständige die Listen mit Wörtern vom Zettel.
In jeder Liste müssen sich die Wörter reimen.

Markiere für jede Liste das passende Lautschriftsymbol.

hear here ~~lot~~ meat meet
not share street there what where

	1	2	3	4
	hot	clear	chair	eat
eə				
ɒ	lot (ɒ circled)	______	______	______
iː	______	______	______	______
ɪə	______	near	______	______

Ordne das Wort in Lautschrift dem englischen Wort zu.

1	lɒt	because	4	'zɪərəʊ	real	7	'peərənts	hair	10	pliːz	CD
2	wɒʃ	lot	5	rɪəl	year	8	weə	parents	11	swiːt	please
3	bɪ'kɒz	wash	6	jɪə	zero	9	heə	wear	12	siː'diː	sweet

6 Picture puzzle

Finde sieben weitere Dinge.

1 train
2 ______________
3 ______________
4 ______________

5 ______________
6 ______________
7 ______________
8 ______________

7 Word search

Die deutschen Übersetzungen für die Wörter in der Box sind in dem Apfel versteckt. Du musst in drei Richtungen suchen. (↓ → ↘)

~~1~~ paint	11 jug
2 autumn	12 both
3 ship	13 expensive
4 rehearsal	14 station
5 group	15 wait
6 use	16 hide
7 terrible	17 hole
8 sound	18 prize
9 ticket	19 short
10 cinema	20 bottle

8 Bits and pieces

Wenn man die Bruchstücke richtig zusammensetzt, ergeben sich zehn Wörter, die du in den vorherigen Units gelernt hast. Finde sie und übersetze sie ins Deutsche.

~~les~~	mate
mor	vous
ner	~~son~~
class	day
birth	ning

1 Unterrichtsstunde
2 ____
3 ____
4 ____
5 ____

week	vorced
bas	cause
tor	ket
be	end
di	toise

6 ____
7 ____
8 ____
9 ____
10 ____

9 Scrambled words

Setze die Buchstaben richtig zusammen und füge sie in die passende Lücke ein.

1 Dan and Jo watched TV yesterday ____ .
2 Ananda ____ hockey ____ Saturday.
3 The band ____ for the show ____ afternoon.
4 Sophie ____ her friends to a party two weeks ____ .
5 I ____ my mum in the kitchen at the ____ .
6 We ____ at a great show last ____ .

~~awchedt~~	envigne
aplyde	ltsa
pastridec	tesyeryad
nivtide	oag
hedlep	kenweed
rewe	thmon

New words ▸ p. 88

Ich bin der **König** der Piraten.	I'm the Pirate ________________ .
Wo ist mein **Tagebuch**?	Where's my ____________________ ?
Gestern **hatten** wir unsere Probe für die Show.	Yesterday we __________ our rehearsal for the show.
„Die Probe war albern," **sagte** Jo.	'The rehearsal was silly,' Jo ______________ .
Bitte **seid** nicht **sauer** mit mir.	Please don't ____________________ with me.
Gestern **sah** ich Herrn Kingsley im Park.	Yesterday I __________ Mr Kingsley in the park.
Ich bin **heute Morgen** spät aufgestanden.	I got up late ____________________________ .

10 Word mix

Bringe die Wörter in die richtige Reihenfolge.

1 of a nice very photo Dan. Here's. Here's a very nice photo of Dan.

2 painting ship. He's pirate a ______________________________

3 Jo too? in Is the photo ______________________________

4 this No, but in photo. he's ______________________________

5 Choir. singing the in He's Junior ______________________________

6 they Are show? the rehearsing for ______________________________

7 evening. tomorrow Yes, starts it ______________________________

11 What are the words?

a) *Finde in den Ziegelsteinen die Gegensätze zu den Wörtern in der Liste.*

big	small
easy	__________
full	__________
interesting	__________
long	__________
loud	__________
terrible	__________

b) *Vervollständige die Sätze mit einem der beiden Wörter aus den Wortpaaren in der Liste.*

1 It's a big school – there are 1,800 students.

2 I can't do this exercise – it isn't very __________ .

3 I'd like some more milk. My glass is __________ !

4 This book is too ______________ to read.

5 Twenty pages! That's a very __________ essay.

6 Be __________ , please. The baby is in bed.

7 I really hated that film. It was ____________ .

New words ▸ *pp. 89 – 95*

Natürlich **haben wir nicht gesungen**.	We ______________________, of course.
Wir **blieben** zu Hause.	We ______________ at home.
Ich lebe gern in einer **Großstadt**.	I like living in a ____________.
Es gibt hier viele **Museen**.	There are lots of _________________ here.
Bist du gestern ins Kino **gegangen**?	____________________ to the cinema yesterday?
Heute ist ein **besonderer** Tag für mich.	Today is a __________________ day for me.
Ich warte auf einen **Telefonanruf**.	I'm waiting for a _____________________.
Mein **bester** Freund will mich anrufen.	My ____________ friend wants to call me.
Ich habe heute **zusätzlich** Hausaufgaben auf.	I've got _____________ homework today.
Ich muss Wörter mit vier **Silben** finden,	I have to find words with four _________________,
... einen **Bericht über** die Show schreiben	... write a _______________________ the show
... und einen **Elefanten** für Biologie zeichnen.	... and draw an _________________ for Biology.

12 Word snake

Zwölf deutsche Wörter sind in der Schlange versteckt.
Schreibe die englischen Übersetzungen auf.

1 practise
2 ______________
3 ______________
4 ______________
5 ______________
6 ______________
7 ______________
8 ______________
9 ______________
10 ______________
11 ______________
12 ______________

Finde aus den zwölf Wörtern sechs, die in die Lücken passen.

1 I practise the piano every day.
2 I'm sorry – I made a ______________.
3 Can you buy a ______________ for the show?
4 We have to get off the ______________ here.
5 Please write a ______________ on the show.
6 I stayed at home ______________.

New words ▸ pp. 96 – 98

Es war eine **dunkle** und **windige** Nacht.	It was a ______________ and _______________ night.
Der **Wind** war schrecklich.	The ______________ was terrible.
Unsere Katze ist sehr **jung** – vier Wochen alt.	Our cat is very _________________ – four weeks old.
Habt ihr **viele** Haustiere?	Have you got ______________ pets?
Wie viele Menschen sind in diesem Zimmer?	________________________ people are in this room?
Vier Männer **töteten** den Piraten.	Four men ___________________ the pirate.
Männer, wir segeln **heute Nacht**.	We sail _____________________ , men.
Sie segelten sechs **Tage lang**.	They sailed __________ six ______________ .
Ich weiß, **dass** sie **Angst hatten**.	I know ____________ they ______________________ .
Endlich kam die Polizei.	______________________ the police came.
Ich bin heute sehr **müde**.	I'm very _______________ today.
Ich will **bald** ins Bett gehen.	I want to go to bed ______________ .
Sei ruhig! Sophie **schläft** noch.	Be quiet! Sophie ________ still __________________ .
Ich sah sie, **als** ich in das Zimmer kam.	I saw her ______________ I came into the room.
Sie sah so **schön** aus an diesem Abend.	She looked so ______________________ that evening.
Bitte gib mir eine **klare** Antwort.	Please give me a ________________ answer.
In den Ferien fahren wir immer ans **Meer**.	We always go to the ___________ in the holidays.
Mach bitte das Fenster zu – **ich friere**.	Please close the window – ______________________ .
Dieses Zimmer ist sehr **kalt**.	This room is very ______________ .
Müssen wir auf dem **Fußboden** schlafen?	Do we have to sleep on the _______________ ?

13 Word pairs

Welche Wörter passen zueinander?

14 Crossword

Across →

1 Another word for 'child' (3)
3 German: Großstadt / English: ★ (4)
5 We can ★ the front door red or green. (5)
8 The day before today (9)
12 In summer we often swim in the ★. (3)
14 You need them to hear. (4)
16 Can I have the ★ of orange juice? (3)
18 We have to ★ a name for our new dog. (6)
20 Why don't we go to the sports ★? (6)
21 What's the ★ of her new book? (5)
25 Listen! Can you ★ that noise? (4)
27 You can learn lots of ★ in Wordmaster. (5)
28 There's a great ★ for the best project. (5)
29 You ★ a glass to drink water. (3)

Down ↓

2 You write notes about the day in a ★. (5)
4 Where are my shoes? I can't see ★. (4)
6 Your feet have got ten ★. (4)
7 Go ★ please – I haven't got time for you. (4)
8 Opposite of 'old' (5)
9 We have to get off the train at the next ★. (7)
10 Please close the front ★ – it's cold outside. (4)
11 The pen is on the ★ – under the armchair. (5)
13 Opposite of 'inside' (7)
14 A nice thing for your ear (7)
15 Our play has got four ★. (6)
17 Opposite of 'down' (2)
19 Opposite of 'long' (5)
20 Polly the parrot is in her ★. (4)
22 Why do I have to ★ my room? (4)
23 You use it when you wash your hands. (4)
24 Some people together (5)
26 You need them to see. (4)
27 My grandfather played football ★ he was young. (4)

New words ▸ pp. 100 – 101

Lebst du auch in einer **Kleinstadt**?	Do you live in a ______________ too?
Nein, meine Eltern und ich leben in einem **Dorf**.	No, my parents and I live in a ___________________ .
Die **Kirche** dort ist sehr alt.	The ___________________ there is very old.
Sie ist **in der Nähe von** dem alten **Turm**.	It's ______________ the old _________________ .
Wir können dort **ein Picknick machen**.	We can _________________________________ there.
Der Bus zum nächsten Bahnhof ist **kostenlos**.	The bus to the next station is ______________ .
Ich wohne in der Nähe von der alten **Brücke**.	I live near the old ____________________ .
Willst du unsere Stadt **erkunden**?	Do you want to ______________________ our town?
Viel **Spaß** in unserer Stadt!	Have __________ in our town!
Hier ist alles sehr **billig**.	Everything is very _________________ here.
Ist der **Preis** für die Eintrittkarte okay?	Is the _________________ for the ticket OK?

1 Fun or funny?

Ordne die deutschen Sätze den englischen zu. Vervollständige die englischen Sätze.

1 Du gehst zu Ananda? Viel Spaß!	☐	*a* Then we watched a ___________ film.
2 Hat es bei Ananda Spaß gemacht?	1	*b* You're going to Ananda's? _______ _______!
3 Ja. Dilip hat uns eine witzige Geschichte erzählt.	☐	*c* Yes. Dilip told us a __________ story.
4 Er hat sein Gesicht angemalt – nur zum Spaß.	☐	*d* Was it _________ at Ananda's?
5 Dann haben wir einen lustigen Film gesehen.	☐	*e* He painted his face – just _______________

2 Spot the mistakes

In jedem Satz sind zwei Fehler. Unterstreiche und korrigiere sie.

1 I life in a village near Bristol. Its very nice there.	live	________________
2 There's a old church near me home – and a nice park.	________________	________________
3 You can sit unter a tree, walk or play – and it's all frie!	________________	________________
4 In Park Street you can go shoping and meet freinds.	________________	________________
5 Let's have a picknick in the parck.	________________	________________

New words ▸ p. 102

Jede Gruppe **muss** ein anderes Thema wählen.	________ group ________ choose a different topic.
Schreibt eure Namen in die linke **Ecke**.	Write your names in the left ____________ .
Einigt euch auf das beste Bild.	________________ the best picture.
Schreib es in die **Mitte des** Arbeitsblattes.	Write it in the ________________ worksheet.
Wir würden gerne zur **Bücherei** gehen.	We'd like to go to the ____________ .
Was ist der nächste **Schritt**?	What's the next __________ ?

3 Word snail

Übersetze die Wörter ins Englische. Trage die englischen Wörter in die Wortschnecke ein. Die Anfangsbuchstaben in der Schnecke helfen dir. Finde das geheime Wort.

4 Opposites

Löse die Buchstabenrätsel, um Gegenteile zu finden.

~~dolc~~ nwe rghit dol
wneitr nem nowd glon

semumr nemow yngou
pu ~~tho~~ shtro worng lod

cold – hot

Finde sechs Wörter aus der Liste der Gegenteile, die in die Lücken passen.

1 It's often very cold in January.

2 I hate winter, but I like ____________ .

3 ____________ often wear dresses.

4 How ____________ is your essay?

5 It's very ____________ – only one page.

6 Is this answer ____________ or wrong?

New words ▸ *p. 103*

Warum **flüstert** ihr zwei?	Why ________ you two ____________________?
Ist die Musik zu **laut**?	Is the music too __________?
Ich kann ein paar **Fotos** vom Baby **machen**.	I can __________ some ____________ of the baby.
Die Kamera liegt **dort drüben**.	The camera is ______________________.
Ich mag dein Foto, aber mein Foto ist **besser**.	I like your photo, but my photo is ______________.
Die beiden Bilder sehen **gleich** aus.	Both pictures look ____________________.
Wir haben beide **dieselbe** Kamera.	We've both got ____________________ camera.
Siehst du **jene** Bilder dort drüben?	Do you see ____________ pictures over there?
Sophie **lächelte**, als sie Fotos sah.	Sophie ________________ when she saw the photos.

5 Lost words

Vervollständige die Sätze mit Wörtern aus dem Tausendfüßler.

1 They can't agree on______ a title for their project.

2 'Smile please. I'd like to take a photo ________ you.'

3 'Don't worry __________ me. I'll be OK.'

4 'You're late again. I always have to wait __________ you.'

5 'I don't like the colour. Can I try ________ another?'

6 'You can come ________ our party too, if you like!'

7 'He really loves books __________ carrots.'

8 'Do you think the cat is afraid ________ us?'

New words ▸ pp. 104 – 105

Ich kann den **Klebstoff** nicht finden.	I can't find the ________________ .
Warum **murrst** du?	Why __________ you ______________________ ?
Ich muss noch meine **Präsentation** üben.	I still have to practise my ______________________ .
Wir machen ein Projekt über die **Innenstadt**.	We're doing a project on the ____________________ .
Ich mag euer Poster **aus vielen Gründen**.	I like your poster ______________________________ .
Ich möchte über meine Stadt sprechen.	______________________ to talk about my town.

6 Pronunciation

Vervollständige die Listen mit Wörtern vom Zettel. In jeder Liste müssen sich die Wörter reimen.

Markiere für jede Liste das passende Lautschriftsymbol.

bread ~~dead~~ down for more
red town saw third word

1 bed ________ dead ________ — aʊ / (e) / ɜː / ɔː

2 brown ________ ________ — aʊ / e / ɜː / ɔː

3 door ________ ________ ________ — aʊ / e / ɜː / ɔː

4 bird ________ ________ — aʊ / e / ɜː / ɔː

Ordne das Wort in Lautschrift dem englischen Wort zu.

1	sed	check	4	'taʊə	how	7	tɔːk	explore	10	'ɜːli	early
2	tʃek	head	5	haʊ	sound	8	wɔːtə	talk	11	ʃɜːt	hurt
3	hed	said	6	saʊnd	tower	9	ɪk'splɔː	water	12	hɜːt	shirt

Ordne die englischen Wörter der Lautschrift zu, um den geheimen Satz zu finden.

ɪf juː dəʊnt nəʊ haʊ tu seɪ ə

If ______ ______ ______ ______ ______ ______ ______

wɜːd tʃek ɪt ɪn ðə 'dɪkʃənri

______ , ______ ______ ______ ______ ______________ .

7 What are the words?

Finde in der Schlange acht Verben und trage sie in die linke Spalte ein.
Finde ihre Vergangenheitsformen in den Blättern und trage sie in die rechte Spalte ein.

Verb	Simple past
see	saw

8 An English-German crossword

Across
2 cold (4)
7 step (7)
8 village (4)
9 middle (5)
12 sea (4)
14 stay (7)
15 choir (4)
16 corner (4)
17 finish (7)

Down
1 better (6)
3 loud (4)
4 autumn (6)
5 reason (5)
6 group (6)
9 grumble (6)
10 diary (8)
11 explore (8)
13 rehearsal (5)
14 soon (4)

New words ▸ pp. 110 – 111

Warte bitte im **Flur**.	Please wait in the ____________ .
Woher weißt du das?	______________________________ that?
Bitte **tu** mir nicht **weh**!	Please don't ____________ me!

9 Numbers and letters: Places in our town

Zu jeder Zahl gehört ein Buchstabe. Finde zuerst die Lösungswörter und dann den „geheimen Satz".

1 It's so hot today. Let's go to the S__ __ __ __ __ __ __ P__ __ __ .
(6 2 9 12 12 9 1 7 — 4 8 8 11)

2 We have to get off the train at the next __ __ __ __ __ __ __ .
(6 3 5 3 9 8 1)

3 The __ __ __ __ __ __ is open on Sundays, but not on other days.
(10 15 14 13 10 15)

4 There are some great books in our __ __ __ __ __ __ __ .
(11 9 16 13 5 13 17)

5 Climb this __ __ __ __ __ and see Bristol!
(3 8 2 18 13)

6 There are lots of interesting old things in the __ __ __ __ __ __ .
(12 14 6 18 14 12)

The secret sentence

__ __ __ __ __ (3 15 18 13 18) __ __ __ (5 13 18) __ __ (6 8) __ __ __ __ (12 5 1 17) __ __ __ __ __ (7 13 18 5 3)

__ __ __ __ __ __ (4 11 5 10 18 6) __ __ (9 1) __ __ __ (8 14 13) __ __ __ __ (3 8 2 1) .

10 Odd word out

Finde und unterstreiche das Wort, das nicht passt.

1 church – library – tower – door

2 pen – cinema – museum – school

3 town – corner – city – village

4 hall – bedroom – kitchen – sea

5 glue – elephant – guinea pig – hamster

6 shout – sing – talk – meet

7 him – she – us – them

8 came – finished – played – nice

9 finish – ran – saw – took

10 him – great – nice – fantastic

11 The fourth word

Welches Wort wird hier gesucht?

1 old – new / never – always

2 rehearse – rehearsal / invite – ______

3 ship – sea / car – ______

4 see – saw / go – ______

5 do – did / sit – ______

6 this – that / these – ______

12 Linking

Verbinde die Satzteile, um Fragen zu bilden. Vervollständige die Antworten.

1 Can	Jack like reading?	Yes, ______
2 Do	Mr Green reading a newspaper?	No, ______
3 Is	Sophie got lots of books?	Yes, ______
4 Does	I go to the library today?	Yes, you can.
5 Are	you have to pay to use the library?	No, ______
6 Has	Dan and Jo at the library today?	No, ______

13 Word mix

Bringe die Wörte in die richtige Reihenfolge.

1 Sophie in time. her free a lot reads — Sophie reads a lot in her free time.

2 about lots books of got horses. She's ______

3 hasn't She any got books football. about ______

4 week. to She library goes the every ______

5 library because it's She the so likes quiet. ______

14 Word friends

Welche Wörter passen zu dem, was die Maus sagt. Finde für jede Mause die zwei richtigen Käsestücke.

15 Word search

Finde im Gitter 30 Wörter, die du in diesem Schuljahr gelernt hast. Die Bilder und die kleinen Bäume helfen dir. Du musst in drei Richtungen suchen. (↓ → ↘)

Welcome

1 Lost words
1 from, *2* about, *3* with, *4* from, *5* in, *6* to, *7* in, *8* about

2 Picture puzzle
Across:
3 football, *4* boy, *7* skateboard, *9* tree
Down:
1 photo, *2* numbers, *4* boat, *5* girl, *6* house, *8* kite

3 Spot the mistakes
1 form: from, nju: new, *2* twinn: twin, They'er: They're, *3* laufh: laugh, heppy: happy, *4* bigg: big, hause: house, *5* empti: empty, iss: is, *6* cann: can, bat: but

4 The fourth word
1 father, *2* pull, *3* girl, *4* empty, *5* you

5 Word snake
1 with – mit, *2* page – Seite, *3* photo – Foto, *4* empty – leer, *5* now – jetzt, *6* pretty – hübsch

6 Word search

W	P	N	O	Y	R	T	A	B	L
O	V	F	N	S	T	I	C	K	J
B	Y	G	U	H	R	P	Q	U	K
E	R	M	P	A	D	S	E	N	O
R	U	L	E	R	Y	P	E	N	X
Z	B	I	D	P	N	L	R	O	C
Q	B	A	G	E	W	A	V	L	A
V	E	P	E	N	C	I	L	S	S
U	R	E	X	E	R	C	I	S	E
M	R	X	V	R	P	O	F	G	U

1 school bag
1 pen
2 pencils
1 pencil sharpener
4 felt tips
1 pencil case
6 exercise books
1 rubber
1 ruler
1 glue stick

7 Scrambled words
1 live, flat, *2* Tomorrow, day, *3* first, school, *4* shop, help, *5* last, holidays, *6* need, for

9 Game corner
blue = 6, orange = 13, yellow = 10, green = 23, brown = 27, black = 50

10 Bits and pieces
1 open – öffnen, *2* partner – Partner, *3* photo – Foto, *4* brother – Bruder, *5* empty – leer, *6* colour – Farbe, *7* mother – Mutter, *8* today – heute, *9* number – Nummer, *10* newspaper – Zeitung, *11* exercise – Übung, *12* welcome – willkommen

11 Odd word out
1 empty, *2* holidays, *3* friend, *4* holidays, *5* me, *6* wheelchair

12 Word partners
1 dad, *2* banana, *3* sister, *4* Berlin, *5* sing, *6* she, *7* blue, *8* pen, *9* Germany, *10* tomorrow

Unit 1

1 There's ... / there are ...
1 There's, *2* Is there, *3* there is, *4* Are there, *5* there aren't, *6* there are

2 Word snail
big, empty, pretty, full, nice, right, new, late, old, great   The secret word: *Prunella*

3 Word search

M	I	L	K	E	U	L	M	P
Q	C	O	M	I	C	Q	A	N
M	A	R	M	A	L	A	D	E
W	R	O	N	G	E	B	Y	R
O	R	T	J	T	V	O	Y	V
R	V	R	N	N	E	X	U	O
D	G	C	F	I	R	S	T	U
S	T	U	D	E	N	T	Y	S
L	E	S	S	O	N	Q	C	T

4 Word mix
1 My book is on the floor.
2 Have you got your sandwich box?
3 The students are at the new school.
4 Are Dan and Jo (Jo and Dan) the mad twins?
5 Is your mum from Bristol?

5 Odd word out
1 enough, *2* breakfast, *3* bad, *4* think, *5* mobile phone, *6* milk, *7* thing, *8* but

6 Numbers and letters: School subjects

French	Music
Science	Biology
Maths	Drama
Art	Geography
History	German

The secret sentence: *I learn English at school – English lessons are great!*

7 Opposites
1 wrong, *2* after, *3* full, *4* push, *5* bad, *6* old, *7* close, *8* girl

8 Word snake: Classroom English
1 toilet, *2* window, *3* work, *4* page, *5* homework, *6* worksheets, *7* sentences, *8* desks, *9* forget, 10 shout

9 What's the word: at or on
1 at, *2* on, *3* at, *4* on, *5* at, *6* At, *7* at, *8* on

10 Bits and pieces
1 lesson, *2* empty, *3* classmate, *4* nervous, *5* picture, *6* enough, *7* student, *8* welcome

11 The fourth word
1 good, *2* her, *3* brother, *4* number, *5* empty, *6* close, *7* our, *8* mother

12 Picture puzzle
1 mobile phone, *2* box, *3* ball, *4* tree, *5* calendar, *6* rubber, *7* girl, *8* pencil, *9* comic, *10* skateboard, *11* parrot

Das ‚geheime Wort': *poltergeist*

13 Scrambled words: Months
1 September, *2* October, *3* April, *4* July, *5* January

The secret word: *Polly*

14 Crossword
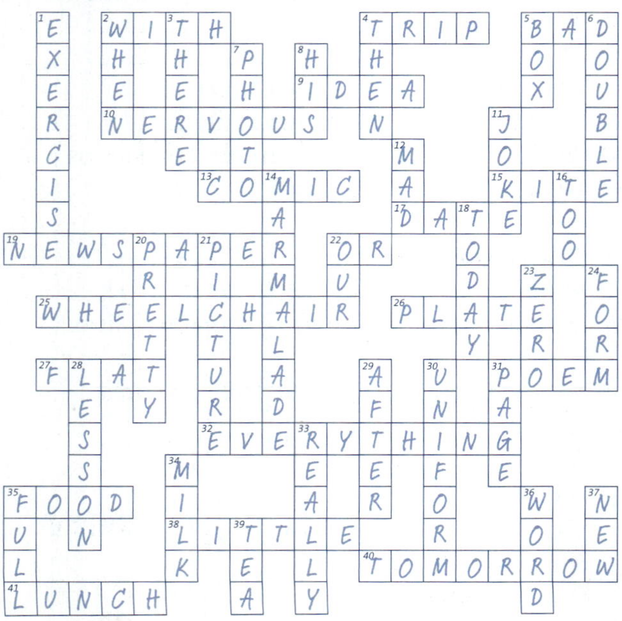

Unit 2

1 Picture puzzle
1 guinea pig, parrot, rabbit, cat, mouse
2 dog, tortoise, bird (oder: budgie), fish, horse

2 Lost words
1 at, in, morning, *2* in, afternoon, *3* on, evening, *4* at, weekend, *5* at, in, evening *6* on, morning

3 Pronunciation
1 date, eight, late, plate (eɪ)
2 do, to, too, two (uː)
3 kite, right, white, write (aɪ)
4 no, know, go, oh (əʊ).

1 great, *2* table, *3* day, *4* who, *5* food, *6* new, *7* nice, *8* like, *9* right, *10* road, *11* home, *12* joke

4 What are the words?
1 please, *2* Sorry?, *3* Here you are, *4* You're welcome

5 Word search
S	O	M	E	T	I	M	E	S
B	R	B	U	O	L	I	E	G
U	C	A	R	R	O	T	B	A
P	X	B	S	T	L	T	U	R
X	Y	A	U	O	K	U	D	D
T	I	S	W	I	B	N	G	E
S	P	K	O	S	K	B	I	N
W	E	E	K	E	N	D	E	M
A	F	T	E	R	N	O	O	N

6 Word groups
school: timetable, classmate, board, PE
family: cousin, Grandma, aunt, grandchild
pets: parrot, tortoise, rabbit, budgie

7 Plurals
1 days, *2* spies, *3* babies, *4* essays, *5* boys, *6* families

8 The fourth word
1 cage, *2* bowl, *3* teeth, *4* difficult, *5* television / TV, *6* aunt, *7* married, *8* letter

9 Scrambled words
1 evenings, family, *2* sits, armchair, *3* children, sofa, *4* thing, fridge, *5* put, food, *6* wash, sink, *7* dishwasher, after

10 Linking

1 **Has Sheeba got** a basket in the kitchen? – Yes, **she has.**
2 **Is Jo** in Ananda's form? – Yes **he is.**
3 **Is Polly a** hamster? – No, **she isn't.**
4 **Has Wanda** got water in her bowl? – Yes, **she has.**
5 **Are Anne and Mark** Sophie's cousins? – No, **they aren't.**

11 Picture crossword

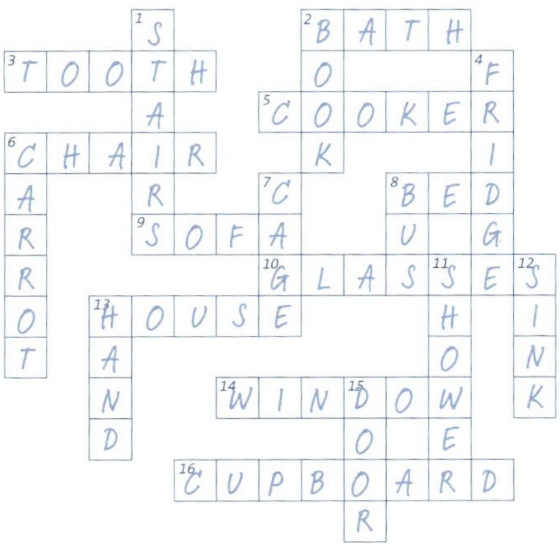

12 Word snail

new, clever, nice, ready, interesting, black, easy, married, empty, boring, dead, difficult

The secret word: *weekend*

Unit 3

1 Scrambled words: Sports

1 badminton, 2 table tennis, 3 football, 4 swimming, 5 volleyball

2 Word partners

go: riding, **do:** sport, judo,
play: volleyball, the guitar,
collect: models, stamps, **make:** models

3 Lost words

1 of, 2 to, 3 at, 4 about, 5 for

4 Word snake

1 Schuhe, 2 Jeans, 3 Hemd, 4 Shorts, 5 Kleid, 6 Größe, 7 Socken, 8 Stiefel, 9 Sport, 10 Farbe

5 Spot the mistakes

1 yu: you, doghter: daughter,
2 Dos: Does, schu: shoe,
3 laik: like, calour: colour,
4 verry: very, trei: try,
5 wont: want, wheit: white,
6 Yu: You, teek: take

6 Word search

V	M	A	S	I	Z	E	G	B	X
Z	P	S	U	L	L	P	N	T	U
A	R	K	R	D	W	I	N	X	S
L	O	Y	W	H	E	A	D	E	T
O	J	G	B	W	A	N	T	F	A
N	E	I	G	H	B	O	U	R	M
E	C	V	D	R	E	D	Z	E	P
Q	T	O	P	X	X	Y	O	E	W

7 Picture puzzle

1 guitar, 2 stamp, 3 kite, 4 cage, 5 piano, 6 football, 7 card, 8 armchair, 9 basket

8 Numbers and letters

1 night, bed,
2 head, always,
3 matches, boring,
4 answer,
5 bike, often

The secret sentence: *I don't really like my new tennis shoes.*

9 Word mix

1 What do most people do in their free time?
2 On Wednesdays Jack's dad plays basketball.
3 Jack doesn't play basketball or do yoga.
4 I have to lay the table for dinner.
5 Why does dad have to play basketball?

10 Odd word out

1 music, 2 shop assistant, 3 fit, 4 hobby, 5 size, 6 walk

11 Pronunciation

1 packet, 2 take, 3 name, 4 that, 5 make, 6 dad

12 Word web

1 kite, 2 page, 3 nice, 4 here, 5 more, 6 date, 7 home, 8 cage, 9 face, 10 live, 11 shoe, 12 size, 13 free, 14 some

13 Word friends

1 **know:** the answer, Dan and Jo
2 **have:** breakfast, a shower
3 **try on:** the shoes, the jeans
4 **ask:** a question, the teacher

2 Spot the mistakes
1 life: live, Its: It's, *2* a: an (old), me: my, *3* unter: under, frie: free, *4* shoping: shopping, freinds: friends, *5* picknick: picnic, parck: park

3 Word snail
bridge, tower, ship, village, church, museum, city, library, room, flat

The secret word: *Bristol*

4 Opposites
cold–hot, new–old, right–wrong, old–young, winter–summer, men–women, down–up, long–short

1 cold, *2* summer, *3* Women, *4* long, *5* short, *6* right

5 Lost words
1 on, *2* of, *3* about, *4* for, *5* on, *6* to, *7* about, *8* of

6 Pronunciation
1 bed, bread, dead, red (e)
2 brown, down, town (aʊ)
3 door, for, more, saw (ɔː)
4 bird, third, word (ɜː).

1 said, *2* check, *3* head, *4* tower, *5* how, *6* sound, *7* talk, *8* water, *9* explore, *10* early, *11* shirt, *12* hurt

If you don't know how to say a word, check it in the dictionary.

7 What are the words?
see–saw, come–came, run–ran, make–made, take–took, say–said, sit–sat, get up–got up

8 An English-German crossword

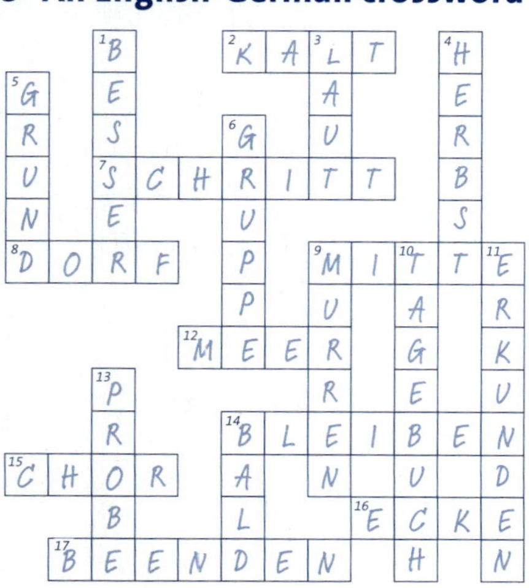

9 Numbers and letters: Places in our town
1 swimming pool, *2* station, *3* church, *4* library, *5* tower, *6* museum

The secret sentence: *There are so many great places in our town.*

10 Odd word out
1 door, *2* pen, *3* corner, *4* sea, *5* glue, *6* meet, *7* she, *8* nice, *9* finish, *10* him

11 The fourth word
1 always, *2* invitation, *3* road, *4* went, *5* sat, *6* those

12 Linking
1 **Can** I go to the library today? – Yes, **you can**.
2 **Do** you have to pay to use the library? – No, **you don't**.
3 **Is** Mr Green reading a newspaper? – No, **he isn't**.
4 **Does** Jack like reading? – Yes, **he does**.
5 **Are** Dan and Jo at the library today? – No, **they aren't**.
6 **Has** Sophie got lots of books? – Yes, **she has**.

13 Word mix
1 Sophie reads a lot in her free time.
2 She's got lots of books about horses.
3 She hasn't got any books about football.
4 She goes to the library every week.
5 She likes the library because it's so quiet.

14 Word friends
1 **get:** off the train, home at six o'clock, *2* **look:** great, at the picture, *3* **make:** a mess, a cake, *4* **take:** photos, notes

15 Word search

14 Crossword

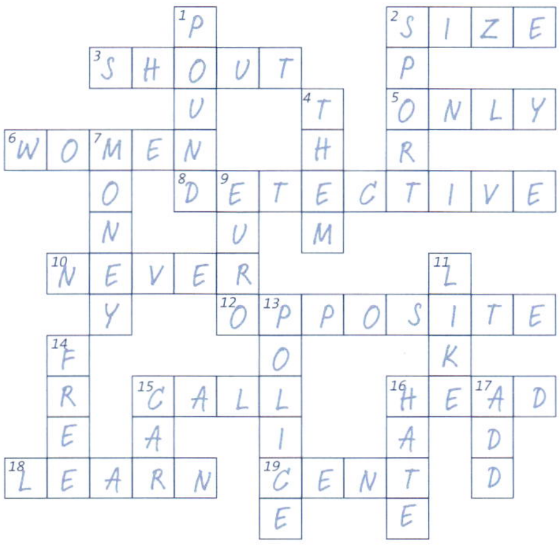

Unit 4

1 Word search

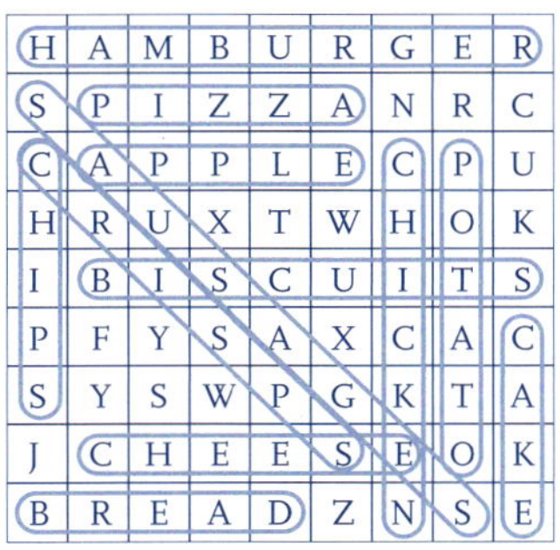

2 What are the words?

1 a plate of chips, *2* a bowl of cornflakes, *3* a packet of crisps, *4* a basket of apples, *5* a piece of pizza, *6* a bottle of orange juice

3 Odd word out

1 euro, *2* glass, *3* milk, *4* ball, *5* top, *6* grandchild

4 Opposites

1 long, *2* early, *3* upstairs, *4* without, *5* open, *6* day

5 Word snail

lemonade, funny, present, bottle, crisps, earring, watch, cheese, dress, soap, holidays

The secret words: *My birthday*

6 Spot the mistakes

1 <u>has:</u> have, <u>Sophies:</u> Sophie's,
2 <u>doesn't:</u> don't, <u>have:</u> has,
3 <u>like:</u> likes, <u>book:</u> books

7 Word groups

1 bath, dishwasher, kitchen, fridge, bedroom, cupboard, armchair, sofa, sink
2 brother, cousin, parents, mother, uncle, grandpa
3 essay, classmate, glue stick, teacher, ruler, pencil case, break, rubber, students, exercise book, PE, lesson
4 meat, chicken, potatoes, cheese, biscuits, cake, lemonade, fruit, marmalade, chocolate
5 shirt, dress, top, shoes, shorts, boots, sweatshirt

8 Lost words

1 for, about, *2* to, *3* for, *4* of, *5* in, *6* on

9 An English-German crossword

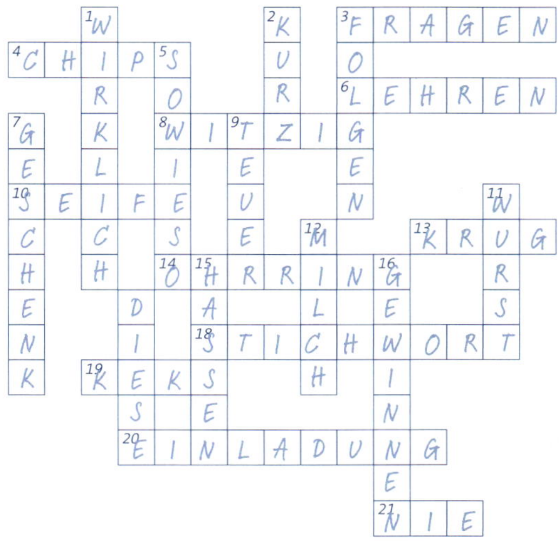

10 What's this

1 hair, *2* mouth (oder: teeth), *3* nose, *4* hand, *5* leg, *6* foot, *7* toe, *8* eye, *9* ear, *10* face, *11* shoulder, *12* finger, *13* arm, *14* knee

11 Word partners

1 arm + chair, armchair, Sessel,
2 basket + ball, basketball, Basketball,
3 bath + room, bathroom, Badezimmer,
4 class + room, classroom, Klassenzimmer,
5 door + bell, doorbell, Türklingel,
6 down + stairs, downstairs, unten / nach unten,
7 every + thing, everything, alles,
8 foot + ball, football, Fußball,
9 home + work, homework, Hausaufgaben,
10 week + end, weekend, Wochenende

12 Scrambled words

1 glass, *2* hear, *3* another, *4* door, *5* away, *6* earrings, *7* parcel, *8* chips, *9* prize, *10* music

The secret word: *sandwiches*

Unit 5

1 Odd word out
1 night, *2* sing, *3* today, *4* hutch, *5* dancing

2 The fourth word
1 pound, *2* rehearsal, *3* ear, *4* down, *5* drink

3 Word web
1 water, *2* colour, *3* paper, *4* answer, *5* dinner, *6* later, *7* winter, *8* junior, *9* choir, *10* number, *11* chair, *12* guitar, *13* finger, *14* sister

4 Spot the mistakes
1 <u>gud</u> good, <u>jesterday:</u> yesterday, *2* <u>childrens:</u> children, <u>vor:</u> for, *3* <u>programm:</u> programme, <u>saunds:</u> sounds, *4* <u>waite:</u> wait, <u>too:</u> to

5 Pronunciation
1 hot, lot, not, what (ɒ)
2 clear, hear, here, near (ɪə)
3 chair, share, there, where (eə)
4 eat, meat, meet, street (iː).

1 lot, *2* wash, *3* because, *4* zero, *5* real, *6* year, *7* parents, *8* wear, *9* hair, *10* please, *11* sweet, *12* CD

6 Picture puzzle
1 train, *2* door, *3* jug, *4* roll, *5* parcel, *6* ship, *7* watch, *8* sausage

7 Word search

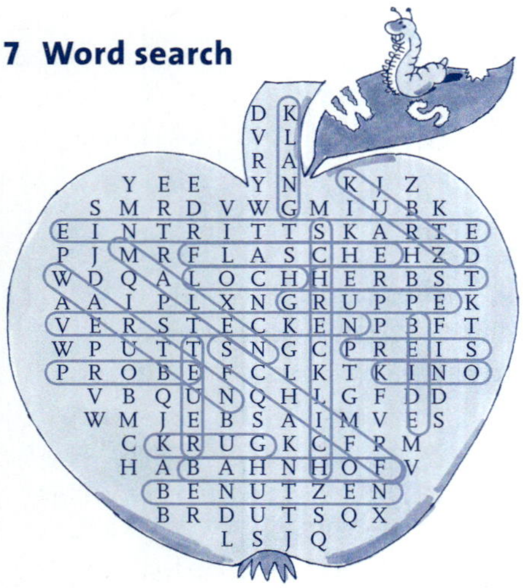

8 Bits and pieces
1 lesson / Unterrichtsstunde, *2* morning / Morgen, *3* nervous / nervös, *4* classmate / Klassenkamerad, *5* birthday / Geburtstag, *6* weekend / Wochenende, *7* basket / Korb, *8* tortoise / Schildkröte, *9* because / weil, *10* divorced / geschieden

9 Scrambled words
1 watched, evening, *2* played, last, *3* practised, yesterday, *4* invited, ago, *5* helped, weekend, *6* were, month

10 Word mix
1 Here's a very nice photo of Dan. *2* He's painting a pirate ship. *3* Is Jo in the photo too? *4* No, but he's in this photo. *5* He's singing in the Junior Choir. *6* Are they rehearsing for the show? *7* Yes, it starts tomorrow evening.

11 What are the words?
a) small, difficult, empty, boring, short, quiet, great

b) *1* big, *2* easy, *3* empty, *4* boring, *5* long, *6* quiet, *7* terrible

12 Word snake
1 practise, *2* city, *3* ship, *4* yesterday, *5* train, *6* ticket, *7* bring, *8* parcel, *9* hide, *10* report, *11* mistake, *12* doorbell

1 practise, *2* mistake, *3* ticket, *4* train, *5* report, *6* yesterday

13 Word pairs
hot: go swimming, **tired:** sleep **funny:** laugh, **scared:** run away, **hungry:** eat, **cold:** stay inside **late:** hurry up

14 Crossword

Unit 6

1 Fun or funny
1 b Have fun, *2 d* fun, *3 c* funny, *4 e* for fun, *5 a* funny